Poker

Everything You Need to Know About Poker from Beginner to Expert

Ian Dunross

Legal Notice:

This book is copyright protected. This is only for personal use. You cannot amend, distribute, sell, use, quote or paraphrase any part or the content within this book without the consent of the author or copyright owner. Legal action will be pursued if this is breached.

Disclaimer Notice:

Please note the information contained within this document is for educational and entertainment purposes only. Every attempt has been made to provide accurate, up to date and reliable complete information. No warranties of any kind are expressed or implied. Readers acknowledge that the author is not engaging in the rendering of legal, financial, medical or professional advice.

Table of Contents

Introduction

I want to thank you and congratulate you for purchasing the book, "Poker: A few tips and tricks on how to get better at the game of poker and make a lot of money ". This book provides you with a good amount of knowledge on a game that was devised to deceive the best – Poker. This is a game that is both challenging and addictive.

There are a variety of versions of Poker available across the world. However, the basic principle is that you use five of the best cards that you have to make your hand. Every version of poker uses the regular 52-card deck. It starts with the number two and all the way up to the number ten. It consists of Aces, Jacks, Kings and Queens of the four different suits – Clubs, Spades, hearts and Diamonds. There are thirteen cards to each suit.

The objective of the game is to win the money. This is the money that is collected throughout the game in a pot that is kept at the center of the table. The players place their bets when they believe that they have the best hand. They might also lay their cards down when they believe that they have to give up ensuring that they get themselves a better hand.

Experts have always said that poker is a game of people. This game deals with understanding your opponents and trying to read and understand their game. There is a certain level of luck that is involved. However, the game solely depends on how well you understand your opponent. Your analysis is what helps you win the game and the money in the pot.

If you are a beginner, you might have never understood the essence of the game. The best way to help you understand the game is by opening an account online. You will have to pay attention to your opponents when you do choose to play with people. Poker can be a very trying game, but once you master the art, you can be sure to have an immense amount of fun!

Once you begin, you will not want to give up! All the best! I hope you enjoy the book.

Chapter 1
The Basics of Poker

When you look at learning a new form of art or a new game, you prefer to understand where the game or art comes from. This chapter covers all you need to know about what poker is and also leaves you with a little bit of its history!

Poker is the national card game of the United States of America! The game has become very popular over the last few decades. From the south of the United States, to the north, maybe even in Alaska, you could find a game in progress at this very second. You can find the Native Americans playing poker. There are chances that a person on a boat could be hosting a poker party. You could play poker on the dining table, or in the card rooms at the clubs near home. You could also play poker in Casinos and Mega clubs where there could be another hundred games in progress.

This book is a book for beginners – people who have never played poker before. If you have always played poker at home, you can learn about how to play the game in casinos or online through this book. If you are a person who has played the game for ages, you could use this book to jog your memory of the rules and the etiquette that you need to follow.

The American dream and Poker

Every person who plays poker or has wanted to learn about poker finds that poker is the one of the main reasons why they love or appreciate the American culture. The Americans have spent a great deal of time in setting the game up. They spent close to 220 years to identify the rules of the game and to make it an important part of their culture. It is rightly called the American dream. A person who is willing to work hard or someone who has the eye for the right moves will always triumph! This has now become the anthem for people all across the world!

Poker has always seemed to be such a simple game to most people. They have the belief that anybody can play the game well. But, this is far from the truth. You may be able to learn the rules very quickly. But, it takes time to ensure that you win every single time that you play the game. A person who is willing to make the effort can become a fairly good player. The only way you can succeed at poker is to face it the way you would face life. You will need to face it with your shoulders squared! You have to ensure that you get up before the next person does. Last but not the least; you have to be faster and smarter than the people around you.

The History of Poker

You have read so much about what the game is. You may now have the question of where this game has actually come from! This section clears this up for you.

There are a hundred movies with gunfights and ballads. These movies have convinced people all across the world that poker is essentially a game that originated in America. But, the fact is that the game originated a hundred years ago! It had all started with the Persians. It was said that the Persians played a game that had the similar rules of poker.

The Germans played a game where they constantly bluffed. They called this game Pochen. It was the French that brought their version of the game to New Orleans. They called this game Poque.

Poque was adopted by the people in New Orleans. They gave it the name Poker. It was during the Civil War that the rules of Poker were modified. They allowed the players to draw cards in order to improve their hands. There is another game called Stud Poker, which is very popular today. This game appeared at the same time as Poker.

There are people all over the world who have started to play poker. There are different versions of poker that have been made. These versions started when people began to play the game at home. There will be games going on in the casinos and the game rooms in different parts of the world – United States, Ireland, Austria, England, Holland, Australia, Germany and many other countries as well! The difference between playing at home and playing at these clubs is that you gamble with pennies at home while at the clubs and casinos; you play for hundreds or thousands of dollars.

Well, is poker good for you?

This is a question that may arise in your minds when you think of gambling. Well, poker is not bad for you. You will find your soul enriched. Your intellect will have sharpened itself and your spirit will be healed! Here is the additional bonus; you will find yourself with a fat wallet if you know how to play the game.

The best thing about poker is that you will learn how to face life and reality. You will learn how to deal with a given situation head on. There are quite a few players who ignore the realities that poker brings them into. But these are the people who lose every single game that they play. They are always unable to face the fact that they are the reason why they lose all the time. They convince themselves that it was the dealer who screwed up their chance of winning. They may blame it on their bad luck, albeit it is true that luck does play a role in poker. They will constantly blame the deck of cards if they have to! They will do just about anything to ignore the fact that it was their foolhardy strategy that brought them down.

However, poker can be terrible for you. This will only happen when you do not learn or understand the strategies that underlie the game. When you are learning how to play, you also have to practice. It is only when you practice that you will be able to identify your shortcomings. You do not have to worry anymore! This book will guide you through every step that you will need to master in order to win poker!

It was the British poker player and author, Anthony Holden, who understood why poker was good for you. In his book 'In Big Deal: A Year as a Professional Poker Player' he said that it is at the poker table where a man's character finds itself stripped of what it is. If the players at the table are able to understand him or read him, he is the person to blame. If he is prepared to see himself the way he is or if he is prepared to see himself the way the people at the table see him, he will be the person who has a chance of winning. Otherwise, he will lose all his games till the end of time!

The challenge that you will have to take up is to understand and analyze your character and the strategies that you choose to win the game. If you do this, you give yourself a greater chance at winning at poker. You will, however, need a little bit of talent to understand when it is that you have to fold your cards to win.

Every building needs a foundation. In the same way, to play poker, you will need a foundation. It is only when the foundation is in place that you will proceed to construct your house or a building on it. When you have finished with the building, you will be able to decorate your building and add the little elements that ensure that the building can be called your own. You can never begin to decorate your building before you have fixed the foundation. It is only when this is done that the other elements of the building all into place. This is the purpose of this book. You will be able to identify the elements that you will need to master first in order to win your game. You will be able to understand what it is that you need to know before you begin to play the game! So pay close attention.

Myths of Poker

There are certain myths to poker that have been spread by the non – believers. They fear the fact that they are being ripped off by the game! This section works on clearing these myths. You should remember that poker is not a bad game.

Myth

The person who wins the most number of pots is the winner of the game.

Truth

Consider the following example. There are different types of businesses all over the world. There could be people who have three or four businesses under their names. Is it the number of businesses that determine how rich the person is or the amount they make every year?

It is the same for poker too! The person who has the most money wins the game! You could win a lot of pots, but if you lose the pots that matter most, you are never going to be the winner of the game.

Myth

You must always ensure that you quit when you are way ahead in the game.

Truth

Let us assume that you are a part of the football team at work or at college. You have started to play exceedingly well on the field. Will the coach pull you back now? When it is you who has been scoring the goals? No way! He would continue to let you play on the pretext that the team has the chance to win.

In the same way, you should ensure that you are always ahead in the game. If you are winning then you can always stay ahead.

Myth

You will need to ensure that you give yourself limits. Otherwise you may lose too much of money.

Truth

This is just the other way of saying that you should always quit when you are ahead. The logic here is that, if the game you are playing is working in your favor, you have to continue to play the game. But, if the game has started to go bad, you should pull out. You must do this even if you are winning.

Myth

You need to have a real poker face to win at poker!

Truth

You can be the way you choose to! You have to only remember that you do not let anyone understand the strength of your hand!

Chapter 2
Poker Rules and Etiquette

You have read about what poker is and have also read about the different tips that you can use to excel at the game. But before delving into the deeper aspects of the game, let us understand the rules and etiquettes of the game.

Rules of Poker

1. Every game needs to have a poker supervisor. This is the person who will ensure that there are no disputes during the game. If there is a need for clarification, his word shall be the final. He will have the right to intervene when he deems necessary.

2. Each player is given a set of cards. These cards from the player's hand. It is his duty to protect the hand for

as long as he can. This needs to be done till he is certain that his hand has lost to every other hand at the table.

3. There is a dealer who ensures that the cards are dealt among the players in a fair manner. The players must ensure that their hand is in the view of the dealer. It is the dealer's job to ensure that the rules are complied with.

4. The person who raises the last bet or the last raise will be the first person to show his cards to the players at the table. This has to be done irrespective of which round the game is on. When the players have displayed their cards, the hand that wins has to be shown very clearly across the table.

5. If a player displays the cards in his hand face – up on the table, the dealer will collect the hand. This is done even if the hand has been placed on the table due to an error.

6. It is the player's responsibility to take care of his hand. If he does not do this, he will lose his cards. The player will not have a chance to play in the game if his hand

becomes fouled or if the dealer picks up his hand accidentally.

7. When you are playing poker, you have to ensure that your money is on the table. The dealer must be able to view the money or the chips that you are going to bed when he is dealing with the cards. You cannot use money that you have not placed at the beginning of the game during the game.

8. If there is a person at the table who has low cash or chips, you cannot transfer any of your money to him.

9. Two or more players cannot bet amongst themselves. The bets have to be made in front of all the players and by all the players.

10. You have to converse in the language that every player knows! You cannot talk to each other in different languages during the game.

11. If there is an error that has been made or is about to be made during the progress of the game when awarding the pot of money, the players and the dealer are obligated to speak up!

12. Any player who has been dealt a hand and is seated at the table has to provide the money to the pot if he does

call it. Let us assume that you are at the table and there are four other players with you. You have each raised a bet. You need to ensure that the bet that you have raised goes to the pot from your money. This is an obligation!

13. The rooms where you play poker, whether online or offline are not responsible if you have left any of your money or chips unattended at the table you were playing at. If you do choose to leave the room, the money you have with you has to be accounted for by the supervisor of that room! This is not required for an online poker game. You have to keep a track of the money that you have.

14. There is a minimum amount of money that every player needs to bring in when he is at the table. If a new player wishes to join the game, he must have the minimum amount of money.

15. If there is a player who would want to contest for the amount in the pot, he will have to do so immediately. If the next round of cards is dealt, the cards in the previous round lose their significance. Assume that you have decided to call for the money in the pot

because you believe that you have a good hand. If you do not do that immediately, you will lose your chance to call the money when the next hand is dealt.

16. If a player has decided to fold, check, call or raise through an indication or a statement that he makes verbally, it is binding on the player who is next as well! This is only valid if the indication has been made within the terms of the game. Let us assume that you are the second person who has to play. If the player before you has decided to call or fold or check, you will have to abide by his indication since you are the next player!

17. A player who wins will always win with a lower number of cards. He can never win with a higher number of cards.

Poker Etiquette

You have been told about the rules that you will need to follow when you are playing poker. Let us now look at the etiquette that you will need to maintain.

1. If you are playing online or offline, you have to ensure that the language you use is appropriate. If you are playing in a poker room, you must dress accordingly.

2. A player who has decided to show his winning hand must do it immediately. This means that the person who has called to fold or for the show of cards must do it first.

3. If you have won the game, you cannot ask the other players you have just beaten to show you their hand. That is impolite.

4. Deception is a key attribute to have when you are playing poker. But it is not fair on your part to take a lot of time before you use a strategy that will undoubtedly be used in the game.

5. There are times when a player may not be interested in the pot that has been placed on the table. He must not fold his cards, then even if there has been no bet that has been made. If he folds, he may be giving another player an upper hand over the other players. It is unfair to fold your cards if there are very few people on the table since it may mean that a player gets the upper hand over the other players.

6. If you do choose to make a raise, you have to announce it!

7. If you choose to go all – in, you have to announce that. Every player on the table must know that.

8. When you do choose to fold, you will have to fold your cards face down on the table. This is the only way by which the dealer can maintain a comfortable and fast – pace of play.

9. There may be times when a person may choose to leave the table for some time. If it is going to be for a very long time, it is best to notify the person managing the entire floor.

10. You cannot keep talking about a hand. This is not a good way to protect you during a game.

11. You must never criticize the way a person has played or his hand. This is impolite. For instance, consider that you are playing poker with three other people. Let us assume that you have won the round. You should never make fun of the way another player has done.

12. If you choose to quit the game, you can whenever you want. No player at the table has the right to criticize you.

13. If there is an improper dealing or if the hand has been read incorrectly, the players must immediately notify the dealer.

14. You should never try to look at another player's hand. This is improper etiquette. You should not try to bend or peek when you are playing. If there is a card face – up on the table, you do not have to look away. Every player at the table has already looked at the card. If you do find that you are able to view another player's card, you should tell the dealer immediately.

15. When the dealer is laying the cards around, he cannot be blamed for the hand that you have received. This is because of the fact that he has no control on what card he is going to deal next.

16. If you have begun to discard cards, make sure that you are pushing them slowly towards the muck, or the pile of discarded cards. You should never push these cards towards the dealer.

17. You have to make sure that your actions or your words do not demean or hurt another player. You should never throw the cards you have in your hand. If you do portray any such uncivilized behavior, you will be

suspended from entering the same poker room. There are times when you may have to stop playing poker entirely.

Ian Dunross

Chapter 3
The Objectives of Poker!

You have read through the different rules and etiquette that will need to be maintained when you are playing a game of poker. You have to now be told about the objective of the game!

What is the objective of poker?

It is a pretty obvious question with a pretty obvious answer! The main objective of the game is to win the money! You can do this by capturing the pot. This is the place, which has the bets that are made by the different players during the round that was played, often called the hand.

Every player makes a bet with the hope that he will win the pot. He believes that he has the best hand. This could also be done if the player wishes to give the other players the impression that he has the best hand. That way he could convince his opponents to abandon the cards that they hold.

The next objective is to save the money that you own. It is always good to save and win! You can only save your money when you know when it is that you have to release the cards that you hold. You have to do this when you believe that you are beaten. This is as important as knowing when it is a good time to place a bet. It is a known fact that the top five combinations of cards are the best cards to hold during a round!

For you to be able to do this, you will need to have a plan that has been formulated with care. You will need to maintain a good amount of discipline as well.

Planning and Discipline

There are a few poker players, just a handful to be honest, who are intelligent beyond recognition when it comes to the game! They have a talent like Picasso did. You would never believe this fact if you only heard it! You would have to see it to believe it!

Even if the person was not a genius, he can win! There are a lot of players who have won poker by learning the game. They have made the effort to understand the different aspects of the game. It is good if you have the ability to learn. It is also good if you have the talent. But, that is not the main ingredient that required to succeed at poker.

You do not have to be Beethoven to play the piano, Leonardo da Vinci to paint or Pele to play football! You can do all the above mentioned activities if you did some learning! It is the same when it comes to poker. You need to have a plan and discipline yourself when playing the game.

How do you plot a strategy?

You have read repeatedly that you need to plan. But what must you do? How do you plan a strategy?

When you have decided to win at poker, you will need to ensure that you have a plan to help you learn the game! Twenty or thirty years ago, people learnt how to play poker at different institutions. But these days, there are players who have mastered their game through their experiences. There is a lot of information available on the web and in many books that will help you work on identifying a plan to learn poker. The next chapter provides you with a learning plan that will aid you improve your game.

Discipline

It is not just the knowledge that you possess in the strategies that matter. That is not the only thing that ensures that a player succeeds. It is important that you have impeccable personal characteristics. If you want to succeed, you will need to ensure that you have a certain level of quality in your characteristics along with the knowhow of poker.

There are players who lack self-discipline and have always had a hard time at winning. They find it difficult to win consistently. This is regardless of how they are good with their strategies. Let us assume that there is a player who does not know when he must throw away a hand that has the poorest cards. He will never win. All the knowledge that he has about poker is an absolute waste.

You have to remember that if you have only the knowledge of poker, but have no discipline, the knowledge is worthless. It is only when you learn to play with discipline that you learn how to handle the losses or gains.

When you look at the musician who journeys all over, or the artist who works only once in a day, you aspire to be them. If you can learn to play poker to their level, you will be able to ensure that you win consistently. You do not have to be a world champion to win money at poker! A person who has chosen the life of a journeyman musician learns how to earn his entire income through his profession. If you have half the skill that he does, you will be able to ensure that you do earn a good amount of money through poker. However, if you do go on to be the best player out there, you will be able to ensure that you become a player who wins at poker for the rest of your life!

Number of players

This is an important part to remember! When you play poker, you cannot play by yourself. You do need another layer. In a regular poker game, the number of players usually varies between two and ten. There are certain types of poker where there can only be seven or eight players.

Ian Dunross

Chapter 4
Poker for Amateurs

As we all know, poker is a game of strategy. The skills required to play the game can easily be learned and developed over a period of time. Gaining a basic knowledge of the strategies to be used and the knack of knowing when to bet or when to pull out will help you make a lot of money through the game of poker. It is a rather fun game once you learn how to play it well.

Some basic ideas

Here are a few tips you should keep in mind before you start gambling of any kind, especially poker.

Tip 1: It isn't necessary to play all the time to win more

A very common mistake made by most beginners is the attempt to play every hand. Even when they are dealt a bad hand, they continue to play just because it is a new experience. You need to inculcate patience and you have to know when to fold and when to play. If you do not know when to quit, you will definitely end up losing a lot of money.

Tip 2: When you are dealt a good hand, play it well

In poker, it is more likely that you will be dealt a bad hand rather than a good one. However, when you are dealt a good hand, you need to make as much money off it as possible. This involves luring the other players so that they add money to the pot. The only way to gain from poker is to win bigger pots than you lose.

Tip 3: Do not bluff very often

Bluffing is one of the most important skills needed to be good at the game of poker. It is the process of making the other players fold when you have a bad hand. It can be a lot of fun and makes the game way more interesting, but it is extremely risky. Bluffing requires you to constantly keep betting on the weak hand that you were dealt. If any of the other players calls your bluff, you will end up losing a lot of money.

Tip 4: Know when to fold

Yet another common mistake made by amateurs is that they often refuse to fold just because they have already bet a certain amount of money. Even though they are quite certain that they cannot win the hand, they continue to play just because of the money they placed in the pot. It is better to fold in such situations so as to avoid the loss of more money.

Tip 5: Poker and depression don't go together

A very common misconception is that poker is something a person does when he/she is sad or depressed. Poker is a game that involves strategy and where the player needs to have a good presence of the mind. Being depressed can only distract you and will not allow you to focus during the game. This will only lead to the player incurring massive losses.

Tip 6: Watch your opponents

Another important skill needed to play the game of poker is the ability to read your opponents. You need to familiarize yourself with any and every pattern that your opponents follow. You must also pay close attention to their facial expressions. These can easily give a player away. However, the player may also be putting on a façade in an attempt to pull off a bluff. You have to be wary of all these things and judge accordingly. Watching your opponents play is an integral part of the game and one needs to be good at it in order to master the game of poker.

Tip 7: Observe your opponents!

While playing poker, ensure that you are keeping an eye on your opponents. You have to adapt to the way they are playing. Try to understand the game that your opponent is playing. If you notice that your opponents are playing tight, raise a little more and continuously call, you have to avoid bluffing. When you find that you have a strong and solid hand, raise large amounts. In the same way, when you find that your opponent is very easy and loose, you will have to either call often or change the way you are playing in order to reap larger profits!

Tip 8: Mix up your playing styles and patterns

As you are trying to read your opponents' games, they will also constantly keep an eye on yours. In case you play the same kind of game every hand, at some point of time, one of your opponents will catch you and you will lose the pot. You need to be able to mix up your playing patterns so that you can always surprise your opponents with the calls you make. Keep varying your bet sizes and time patterns. This way, your opponents are more prone to misreading your hand and this increases your chances of winning big.

Tip 9: Don't jump between levels; change gradually

Just because you are winning big at the lower stakes table, doesn't necessarily mean that you will win at the higher stakes. Although the wins at higher stakes are big, losses incurred are massive as well. Even the players at the higher stakes table have more skill; that's the reason they play there. If you do want to change levels, change gradually, increasing your skill at each level you pass.

Tip 10: Mistakes are to be learned from

The cliché that a man who learns from his mistakes is always successful in life applies to poker as well. After you are done playing, analyze your game. Look at the hands that you won and see if you could've somehow won bigger. Look at the hands you lost and check if you should've folded earlier and minimized your losses. This will help you improve your game and you can reap profits.

Tip 11: Play a fair game

You have to always keep in mind that poker is just a game and that in a game, where there are winners, there are also losers. As you keep playing, you will find yourself on both sides. Do not trash talk the other players and gloat when you are winning and do not sulk when you lose.

Tip 12: Know what type of player you are

There are basically two types of players in poker: those who play to win and those who play it as a recreational activity. You need to decide what type of player you are. If you want to play to win, it needs a lot of practice that takes up a lot of your time. Basically, you need to work hard to be good at the game. However, you could just play it occasionally for fun. You need to figure out which of the two you are before you start playing.

Chapter 5
Poker Hand Ratings

In this chapter, we will explore the rankings of different poker hands and this will give you a definitive idea of how to play the game well.

The various hands that you can be dealt in poker are ranked in a certain order. As the rank increases, the chance of you being dealt that hand reduces. Also, the higher the rank, greater is the chances of you winning the round. However, a good hand doesn't guarantee you a victory. If more than one player has the same hand, there are other ways in order to determine who wins the round. As you keep playing the game, all these points will start to make more sense.

Poker Hands

As mentioned earlier, poker is a game of concentration and presence of mind. In addition to these, you need to memorize the poker hand rankings as well. Given below is a list of the poker hands from best to worst. Once again, you have to memorize this order and know what each hand is.

Royal Flush

This is the rarest hand in a game of poker. A Royal Flush is a sequence of cards from ten to the ace and all the cards need to be of the same suit. If two players hold a royal flush (which is highly unlikely), the players share the winnings.

Straight Flush

Another rare hand, a straight flush is a hand comprising of five cards of the same suit in sequence (6, 7, 8, 9, 10 for instance). The example given is called a ten high flush. Higher the card, higher is the ranking, i.e. a Jack high flush beats a ten high flush. An ace high flush is a Royal flush.

Four of a Kind

As the name suggests, a Four of a Kind is a hand comprising of four cards of the same rank (four tens for instance).

Similar to a straight flush, a tie is won by the person with the higher set. If a tie occurs, the winner is decided by the other card held by both players.

Full House

A full house is a hand that consists of a triplet and a pair (three tens and two sevens for instance). A tie is decided by the value of the triplet. If the two players have the same three matching cards, the power of the pair is taken into consideration.

Flush

A flush consists of five cards of the same suit in no particular sequence. All the suits in poker are of equal rank. Ties are settled by the highest ranked card of the flush. If the same high card is shared, the other cards are taken into consideration to decide the winner.

Straight

Straights consist of five cards in sequence from different suits. Again, in case of two or more players having the same straight, the winner is decided by the highest card. Do keep in mind that an Ace can be used as both a low card and a high card for a straight. So A, 2, 3, 4, 5 would be the lowest whereas 10, J, Q, K, A would be the highest.

Three of a Kind

Consists of three cards of the same rank (three tens for instance). Highest card decides the winner if two players have triplets. In case the tie arises due to the same triplet, the highest unrelated card decides the winner.

Two Pair

A Two pair consists of two cards of the same rank, two other cards of the same rank and one card forming two pairs of different kinds. If there is a tie, you cannot ask for a tiebreaker. The player with the same highest pair wins the game. If there are two players who have the same pairs, the next pair is measured. If there are two or more players who have the same pairs, which is highly unlikely, the fifth card is checked!

One Pair

Similar to a two pair, a one pair consists of two cards of the same rank. If two players have pairs, the higher pair wins. If two players have a pair of the same rank, the tie is decided by the unrelated cards. First additional card takes preference over the second and the second takes preference over the third.

High Card

If no player has any of the hands given above, then the winner is decided by the highest card out of the five. If two players have the same highest card, the second card is taken into consideration. If even the second cards are the same, the third is taken into consideration and so on. If all cards match, then the two players split the pot.

Ian Dunross

Chapter 6
Personalities of Players

In this chapter, we will look at the various kinds of player personalities that you will encounter. We will also look at a few tips on how to play each personality in order to win. As you analyze your opponents, you will be able to figure out what type of players they are and you will be able to play them accordingly.

Poker is a game of observation, so the first step to analyzing a player's style is to observe his/her tendencies. This is one of the main factors for success in poker. Every action your opponent takes is important.

The basic poker player personalities

Every poker player can be classified under two factors that define their playing style, in general. They are: tight vs. loose and passive vs. aggressive.

Tight vs. Loose

This distinction can be made by observing how often a player plays his hand. You will understand this better at the end of the chapter.

A player who only plays strong hands is classified as "tight". These types of players generally fold quickly whenever they are dealt a weak hand. Loose poker players will play a vast number of hands, including the weak ones.

The categorization of tight and loose doesn't really tell you much about the style of playing as it does about the selection of hands that the player will play. The style of playing can be figured out by figuring out whether the player is "passive" or "aggressive".

Passive vs. Aggressive

This factor is displayed by a player's nature of play.

Players can be categorized as passive if they play with the fear of losing. They have a very conservative style of playing the game. Aggressive players play with confidence and these are the type of players who bet big money.

It isn't very hard to classify a player as tight or loose and passive or aggressive. Just by watching them play, it becomes apparent what type of a player a person is. The first thing to do is to determine whether the person is a tight or a loose player. Check if he/she folds very often. If they do, they can be categorized as tight. Otherwise, they are loose players. If players call or check often they are passive and if they bet or raise a lot of money they are aggressive players.

The various combinations

There are four possible player personalities that can arise from the above qualities. They are enlisted below:

1. The tight and passive: Fold or call/check often.
2. The tight and aggressive: Fold often but bet big when dealt a good hand.
3. The loose and passive: Play almost every hand and call/check as much as possible.

4. The loose and aggressive: Fold very rarely and bet big money.

Most players don't generally fall into one of these categories perfectly. These categories can be used for initial categorization. Once the game starts, every good player tries to vary their playing styles so as to deceive the other players. You need to analyze the players as they play and change your game accordingly. Blindly going by the above four categories can mislead you and you may end up losing big.

Aggression

In the game of poker, it is advisable to be aggressive. You are not expected to win much if you play a non-aggressive game. Since the essence of the game is to beat your opponents and take their money, aggression is a must.

There are certain situations where deception is a part of the game. Even aggressive players do this from time to time, but it is how they do it, unlike a tight-passive player who only calls when they should be raising, all because from the fear of losing.

The main disadvantage of a passive style is that you only win when you are dealt a good hand. However, a person with an aggressive style can win when he has a bad hand too as he will try to bluff his way out of it and make his opponents fold even though they have better hands.

Which style of playing is the best?

As mentioned above, aggression is an absolute must for a poker player. The question about whether a loose or a tight strategy is better remains. Both can be employed and along the years, both have been known to be winning strategies. A loose and aggressive style is slightly risky and is advisable only for experienced players because when things go south (which is very likely with this style), improvisation is needed which is a skill developed with experience. Hence, for beginners, a tight-aggressive style is perfect. This will also inculcate patience in the player that is another key component in the game of poker.

Once again, emphasis needs to be laid on the fact that no player sticks to his or her style. If they did so, it would be easy to read their moves and they would lose a lot. Every player at a poker table looks to improvise and change his or her game according to the other players. You could revert back to your original playing style sometime later on in the game but you shouldn't make it obvious. You must always keep your opponents on their heels such that they're constantly trying to predict what your next move will be.

Improvising and changing your playing style constantly is something that you will learn as you play the game. So do not feel discouraged that you aren't able to do it right at the beginning. When you start out, play a very conservative game and notice other players and how they play. You will be able to win big in no time at all.

Chapter 7

Bluffing Your Opponents

In this chapter, you will be taken through the art of bluffing, an integral part of the game. This is something that can be easily understood by non-players as well. It is basically the act of making your hand look stronger than it truly is. This will cause your opponents to fold even though, in reality, they have a better hand than you. You will effectively win on weak hands if you can master this technique.

There are five factors that characterize a bluff:

The Opponents

Your opponents are the main factor. If they fall for your bluff and fold, you win the hand. If they call your bluff, you lose. You need to be able to affect your opponents' game style if you want to bluff successfully. It also helps if you can single out a certain opponent to bluff. This increases the chances of your bluff succeeding. Do not try bluffing a passive player who won't bet much money. It's easier to bluff an aggressive (good) player rather than a bad player.

To improve the efficiency of your bluff, you need to take into account the recent form of the other players at the table. If someone has been winning big, he or she becomes an easier target to bluff. On the other hand, someone who has been losing starts playing in a very risky manner and this makes them bad targets.

The style of your game

How your opponents see you as a player also affects your bluff. If they think that you are a tight player, the chances of your bluff succeeding increase because they feel that every bet you make will be on a good hand. If they think you are a loose player, they can easily call your bluff because you would have been calling every hand that you were dealt up to that point.

Strength of the hand (the cards you are dealt)

There are two types of bluffs based on the cards you have in your hand. Pure bluffs occur when you are dealt a hand that has no chance of winning whatsoever unless your opponent folds. These bluffs are extremely risky and need a lot of skill to be played out successfully. Another type of bluff is called a semi-bluff. These bluffs are done when there are chances of your hand strength improving as the game progresses. Basically, these are bluffs with a backup plan. Obviously, a semi-bluff is more efficient than a pure bluff. So, while bluffing, keep the strength of your hand in mind.

Pot Size

Another consideration that has to be made while bluffing is the size of your bet. In order to pull off a perfect bluff, you need to slowly increase your bet size in order to win more from the bluff. If you directly go all in, many people are likely to fold. This does win you the pot, but you do not actually win much. If you can gradually increase the bet and go all in deep into the game, you are more likely to win a huge amount of money with a weak hand. This is a very risky method and you shouldn't look to employ it very often. If, as the game progresses, someone gets a very good hand, he or she will look to stay in the game as long as possible. If the player is aggressive, he might even go all in when you do and he will end up winning the pot. He would have called your bluff unintentionally.

You need to be extremely careful while playing a bluff, as it isn't very reliable. However, if you can master the art of bluffing, you automatically will become a great poker player.

Chapter 8
Observing and Reading Your Opponent

Many beginners think that the ability to read your opponents is something impossible. They feel that reading a player involves predicting the exact two cards in the player's hand. That, however, is a misconception. It is impractical to actually think that it is possible to know the exact two cards in your opponents' hands. The idea is to figure out whether or not the opponent has a strong hand.

This can be done by reading your opponents' moves. You need to be extremely focused on the game in order to read the moves properly. Depending on whether the player keeps calling/checking or whether he is raising the bet constantly can help you figure out the strength of the opponents' hand. You need to be able to adjust your game according to your observations. If someone looks like they have a very strong hand and are certain to win, it is advisable to fold. However, the person might be bluffing so you need to make accurate observations.

The First Law of Hand Reading

The first law of hand reading depends on the player's position in the betting order. The earlier a player's position in the order, the narrower is the range of the cards that he might be holding in his hand. If someone with an early position calls a bet, it is safe to assume that the player has a strong hand. As the position in the order decreases it gets harder to judge what type of cards the player has.

Take a walk in his shoes

When you are reading a situation, you always try to think from the perspective of your opponent. That is what the first law of hand – reading states. While doing this, you have to be careful to avoid making blind assumptions during the play. You might find that the style that your opponent has is very similar to your very own, but that is all it is. It is similar, not the same. Hence your assumptions might not be very accurate.

Another complexity of the game is that you and your opponent might be doing the very same thing at the same time! While the game progresses, you have to identify how your opponent is playing and change your game to help you reap the highest benefits. The game might seem terribly difficult and you might find that mastering it is a tiring ordeal. But playing simple will sadly not help you win!

Identify your opponent's weaknesses

When you being to identify and understand the way your opponent plays, you analyze how they play different combinations – for instance, the top pair with the top kicker. This is a very common play and is always played recklessly. If you find that there is an opponent who goes all out with this combination, you can be sure to win without wasting a drop of sweat. You can easily trap him through a flush or even a two pair. When you observe your opponent, you know what his weaknesses are and will definitely be able to trap them with ease!

Ian Dunross

Chapter 9

21 Secrets to Dominating the Table in a Game of Poker

Learning to play poker is one thing; earning how to play like a pro and dominate any table you play at is another thing entirely. I'm going to share with you 21 secrets on how you too can take the table and walk off with the prize – every time you play.

Keep Records

If you are deadly serious about playing poker for a living and beating the table every time, you must keep detailed records of every game you play. You will never remember your performance for every single game, unless you have a super brain so get yourself a notebook. Write down everything about every game you play so you can go back over it and monitor how you're playing and improving. You might feel a little daft and people might look at you a little strangely to start with but in no time at all, you will have a bestselling book in your hands – your journey from a timid player to pro player who is always winning.

In terms of statistics, the performance data you are collecting can be analyzed later. You can ask yourself questions that are designed to improve your knowledge and your game. Questions like "why did I play that hand in that way?" "Why didn't I play it that way?", "Did I do the right thing with this middle-pair?", "Should I have called my opponents in-play on the last hand for the pot?"

Keeping records isn't just about recording your wins and losses though. It's all about giving you a picture of you as a player, knowing when you played badly and when you played well. You may have won a game but that doesn't mean you played it well! Your records are about being conscious of the choices, the decisions you make at the table on the night. Your records are the difference between staying a timid mouse and becoming a roaring lion.

Play All the Time – Even If You Don't Feel Like Playing

If you are serious about playing poker and winning, you have to play all the time, no matter how much you don't feel like it. There will come a point when you ask yourself if it is worth carrying on, if you have what it takes to be a serious poker player. By serious, I am not talking about not smiling or not talking while playing. By serious, I mean having the commitment to poker, no matter what else is happening. Are you truly aware of the differences between amateurs and pro? Amateurs walk away when things get a tougher but the pro will be there, no matter what. Part of being a pro player and dominating your opponents is showing up even when you are not feeling your best – you still have to play your best though! There are two requirements for a serous poker player – dedication and commitment. If you haven't got one or either of them, you cannot give your all to the game.

Game Selection

Once you have mastered the record keeping and you begin to get good at keeping your score and at winning games, what do you do next? Do you immediately spring up to the high stakes games and put your entire month's winnings down as a bet? Make things easy on yourself. First, decide where you are going to play – online or live poker (or both if you so choose). It could even be a local game place in your area. Talk to any pro player and they will tell you that they started out that way; they pulled their roots out and moved on to where they are now. Much depends on your circumstances – if you have a family life that you don't want to lose, consider playing online – you can win just as much there as you can in a live poker game. Or relocate to where the big games are. Whichever you choose, give it a shot for six months and get a good idea of the environment you are playing in. If you want to play live poker, you need to follow the money. If you want to play online, do your homework. Look at all the sites, join the forums and talk to other players. Watch games, see how other players behave in different limits ad set you a controlled game plan to stick to.

A word of warning for those of you that chooses to follow the money and go the big leagues. You will meet players of a much better caliber than you are. You need to be able to spot them early, not because you are going to battle against them but to find your own spot within the poker hierarchy. Yes, you will come up against these players at some time in the future but your first objective is to find the balance between the limits at the tables and how much money you are prepared to lay down every day. The amount of money you can make playing poker depends on your opponents. It won't take you long to realize that small limits are easy to beat but you won't earn much money compared to the bigger stakes games.

Those big stakes games have one problem though – the players will be much tougher to beat. The real secret is finding the right balance between making enough money and increase how often you win on a regular basis. When you find the limit that is right for you and can beat it, then you can call yourself a pro player. Climb the ladder but do it slowly – the objective isn't to haul in the wins straight away; it's to learn how to do it in a calm and stable manner and consistently.

Learn the Power of Expectations and Statistics

You may have a gut feeling that you are good enough at this game to earn a good living at playing poker but something is holding you back. You don't know for certain if you are a winning player or not. So, the next secret to learn is a technical one. It isn't difficult but it will determine your future. Poker math is very different from the college math you learned, and it's very different from the math learned by kids at Princeton, the kids who see to go crazy afterwards! You don't need to have a "beautiful mind"; you just need to learn some of the useful statistics so that you can calculate your own expectations. One of the most useful tools is to learn the standard deviation – and that isn't quite as complicated as it sounds. All it means is to learn how your game swings. Do you play consistently or is your technique different every time? The higher the standard deviation for each game, the higher the variance and that means more chance of being beaten. The lower the deviation, the less chance there is of a bad streak.

Standard deviation is used to determine how near to your averages you are – or how far in some cases. Keep in mind that your standard variation is different from everyone else's. Your standard deviation will depend on a number of different factors – the way you play, your opponent's style of playing, whether the table is swingy or not. Once you understand how standard deviation works, you will be able to understand how you are playing within your winning average.

Do You Shy Away From Taking Risks?

Let's assume that you are in the middle position, mid stack and you have been dealt pocket tens. The player under the gun has raised by an amount five times the blind and the following player rc-raised a further three times. It's your turn – what do you do? Do you call or do you fold? Do you re-raise? You are going to find yourself in this kind of situation when you become a serious poker player. Ask any pro that you know and you will be given, quite literally, hundreds of different scenarios for that one hand alone! So, how should you play those pocket tens? The answer depends. Really. It depends on how much risk you want to take – after all; we didn't tell you everything about the hand, did we? I didn't tell you how the other players play, what their characteristics are, how long they have been poker players, what size their stacks are, etc. There really isn't a right or a wrong answer to this scenario. It depends on you and your aversion – or not, as the case may be – to risk in each hand that you play.

The way you play determines how you approach each hand. If you are looking for a larger win rate, you need to be an aggressive player. But, do remember the standard deviation. You could choose to be conservative and go for winning one big bet every hour but this would mean having to play longer hours that you would normally.

Learn Your Trade from the Very Best – And Then Beat Them

If you really want to learn to play poker with the best then you have to learn from the best, it's as simple as that. Pick a pro player that you admire, pick two or three and then study how they play. Mimic them. Learn how they strategize every game and watch how their games unfold. Once you understand what they are doing, include their strategies in your own games. Over time, you will develop your own style of play, by using their moves in with your own – in the right places of course. Now try to beat those players at their own game!

Sadly, there are a lot of players who can't balance their poker life with the rest of their life and things end up suffering. To play poker as a pro, is an incredibly lonely life and many sacrifices have to be made if you want to get to the top. Find players who are intuitive and learn from the; learn how they play and how they approach a game. Let me tell you a story about a friend of mine and a pro that he played with on a number of occasions. He's not a high stakes pro, simply an average person who plays part time and makes a reasonable amount of money at it. When my friend watched this man, he saw some amazing things. He saw him fold on a flush in a three-way game because he believed that one of his opponents had a full hand. He folded pocket jacks and pocket kings in another game. Why?

He said that the hand you throw let go is as important as the one you play. He is a very aggressive and relentless payer and he can get out of bad plays in most situations. He commits to the game but never so much that he can't get out. When you play poker, you will come across a wide range of characters but there will only be a few who really stand out. Pick the ones you think you can learn from and hang on to them. That's playing live. It's a different game altogether when you play poker online because you need to work a lot harder to figure out who is good and whom you shouldn't take any tips from. You can do a number of things here – join the forums and talk to people; join a site that offers tutorials and analyze your own game or join a pro site, pay a subscription and let the pros teach you how to play. It's your choice what you do but remember – the most important thing is learning from the best and then being able to beat them later on.

Ask the Right Questions

There are lots of players who simply don't know the right questions to ask. I'm talking about the type of player who keeps complaining that he's constantly being beaten – badly. About the player who keeps on winning with bad plays and calls. We've all been in that situation and, if you are the type of player who needs to ask why lady luck is never on your side, you really need to do a lot more work on your game. If you can't figure out why your aces never hold up when another player wins every time with bullets, it means that you don't have any control of the table.

When you start to ask the wrong questions, you are subtly but surely chipping away at your poker mindset. To be perfectly brutal, you should never ask these questions. All they are achieving is a sense of self-defeat. Instead, you need to change your attitude. When the bad cards come your way, you must acknowledge that you can change the situation; you can change the way the game will end. Instead of blaming circumstances or blaming other players, instead of asking "why does that bad player always win?" ask instead how you can prepare for winning, what you need to do to make sure you win. Be positive instead of negative and focus, not on your losses but on what you need to do to become a better player. To be successful at poker you need skill, courage, and determination and are prepared to keep on going when everything seems to have fallen apart. Build a system that works, improve it, execute it and trust in it. That is how to win at poker.

See Through Each Opponent

You don't need to have x-ray vision for this! What you do need to be able to do is work out how your opponents play. In many cases, when you are a beginner, you will end up playing heads up against the wrong opponent. Think about how often you tried to bluff a player that was considered to be a calling station. You know you shouldn't do it but you do. You know that you need a dead strong hand to win against a calling station who, by the way, is a player who cannot be bluffed. Yet, still you keep on trying to bluff. You have to know your opponents. It is very helpful if you know how to read body language but that really only seems to happen in the movies! Many pro players are able to act out what they want you to see or to show absolutely no emotion whatsoever. So how do you learn to read your opponents?

Watch them. Watch how they play and learn the patterns to their betting. Do they play every single hand or do they discard some? The best thing to do is sit and watch your opponent play in a game that you are not included in. You might just be surprised at what you can see.

Poker is Business, It's Not Personal

So you've been playing poker for several hours without stopping and there is one player at your table who is losing from every direction. At last, he gets dealt pocket aces (you wouldn't know this at the time) and has decided that he will do whatever it takes to win his money back. He slow balled the aces and raised, just enough to get sufficient callers. You are holding a nine and eight of clubs on the button. There are two more callers so you did a few calculations in your head on the pot odds and decided that it wouldn't do any harm to call. The two players before you checked and the losing player flops his pocket aces with the community cars, which are a seven and six, and decides to check as well. You checked and you got your nuts straight on the turn with a five. Your hand is clearly the best but the losing player has gone all in, forcing the others to lay their hands down. You call straight away. The river card didn't help him and your hand is still the best.

The losing player is now so frustrated that he splashes the pot and challenges you to a fight! He keeps on at you, not letting up unless you give him what he wants. So what do you do? You know the answer and you know that the same would be true if the situation were the other way around, although perhaps you wouldn't be challenging your opponent to a duel at dawn! When things like this happen, you have keep your emotion in check and leave your ego behind. It may be easier said than done but, at the end of the day, poker is business and you cannot take the consequences of what happens personally.

If a player on your table is picking on you, is constantly calling your raises, as if he is trying to prove a point, don't give him the satisfaction. If you lose a hand to him and he laughs, ignore it. You are playing to earn money or have some fun, not be drawn into personal vendettas. However, it would be good if you got the opportunity to take his chips from him but only do so when you know you can win – and win big.

Pay Attention at all Times

No doubt, you have seen players who listen to their iPods while playing poker and, while there is nothing that says you shouldn't, you are better off on focusing your entire concentration at the game. You need to be paying full attention, to the game and to the other players. Listen to conversations, watch the players, listen to their commands o each play. You will learn an awful lot, much more than you would if you were listening to your favorite music

Join a Poker Forum or Two

Earlier we mentioned joining poker forums to help you improve your game. Many years ago, those who owned a computer were few and far between and even fewer had access to the Internet. These days we are connected, everywhere we go, through our laptops, desktops, tablets and smartphones. When you play poker, it is important that you have easy access to the internet, to go online and look through all the different poker websites, read all the information you can and find out as much information as you can. You can never have too much knowledge; the problems come when you do not know how to properly apply what you have learned. While you are there sign up to a few poker forums. You'll get involved in lots of chatter, some of it purely social and some of it about poker so learn how to filter what you read and you'll find some of it highly beneficial to your game. New ideas, strategies, techniques, approaches and things to avoid are all learnt in these places so get actively involved and learn.

It's you against them

If you know anything about the natural world, you'll know something about the relationship between the doves and the hawks. The doves are peace-loving birds; expert communicators, diplomatic and they know how to use channels of agreement. The hawks are practical birds. They swoop in without warning to ensure their survival and to deter others from threatening them. In poker, you will find both hawks and doves playing at the same table but they are called fish and sharks instead. The fish is food for the shark and you need to be aiming to be that shark. Poker is not about making friends or reaching amicable agreements. Yes, you should have friends but keep in mind that, whoever is at your table is they friend or stranger, is out to take your money from you. Your mission is to survive and, to do that, you need to take out all the fish; you need to control your gam and the table and bring home the cash. If you don't, your money is going home in someone else's pocket.

Practice Playing Online

When you are so exhausted after a hard day at work that you simply don't have the energy to drive to your game, you get online and you play there. There are no excuses here. If you want to learn to be a pro, if you want to be able to dominate the table, you have to practice. You can't learn to play by just sitting a few games; it will take you thousands of games to get going and you will lose a good proportion of them. But, the more you play and the more experienced you get, the more you will win – and that works online and with live poker games. With live poker, the number of hands dealt is limited but, when you play online, there is no limit – you can play thousands of hands per month. You get the practice (don't forget to fill in your journal) and you will improve. Also, with online poker games, you get an added bonus – statistics and analytics for each had played. You can get an instant replay of the hand and you can see your history. An online site offers brute mathematical force so take advantage and learn hard.

Back to the Records

Sooner or later, you are going to be hit by variance and it will be painful, make no mistake about it. There will come a time in your career where you will wonder if it's all worth it and this experience is different for everyone. It will feel as if there is no point anymore because, no matter what you do, how hard you try, nothing seems to work and you are on a real bad losing streak. The worst thing you can do is brood. Keep on going, following your strategy because you will start to win again. Remember all that record keeping you has been doing? Go back to it, look at it and compare your performance now with then; see what's happening, where things really started to go wrong. Records help to keep you grounded. Talk to other players and you will find that they generally overrate themselves as players. No one likes to admit that they are losing, except for perhaps those that are more intuitive. Keep going with the records, keep them updated. Bear in mind that your mind is somewhat selective about what it processes in terms of information – writing it all down means you can never forget anything you have done and it also means that you can see where you are going wrong.

Read Lots of Books on Poker

Have you ever read a book about poker? And I don't mean a thriller that was set in poker room! Try it; open a book on poker when you are at your card room and you will hear a number of sneers, from people who have been playing for years and don't reckon that a book can teach them anything. These people continually make the same old mistakes, year in, year out. These are the players who are high superstitious at the poker table – lost because they didn't have their lucky shirt/pants on; want a new deck *because the current one is dealing fairly or don't want a particular dealer because he or she is a jinx on the game.

Be very wary of this kind of player – stupidity is highly contagious. Read, get as many books as you can on the subject of poker and learn. Understand what you are reading, let it broaden your perspective a little and don't get confused by all the different strategies in the books. Reading books is the same principle as keeping records – they are a reminder that you really don't know it all and you have a lot to learn still. Books are as much a useful investment as the time you spend playing poker is.

A Word on Aggression

Imagine that you are in a tourist spot, walking with your partner. You are having a nice romantic evening together when, with no warning, a group of men start calling out your girlfriend, telling her she would be better off with them than with you. They throw a few insults in, designed to get your goat up ad provoke you. Now, for the last few years, you have been practicing and have become quite proficient in a deadly martial art. So, what do you do? Do you go headlong into a deadly fight to protect your partner?

You know that, whatever you do in life, wherever you are, you have to pick your fights carefully. That same principle can be applied to a game of poker. That's why Texas Hold' me is called No Limit. Poker gives you an option – to hold 'me or fold 'me. Even if you are being bullied at the table, it doesn't mean you have to bite and retaliate with aggression. It's not shameful to back off especially when it is not tactical to engage your opponent. Be very selective with your aggression; it will get you a long way.

On Tilt

Let's assume you have been dealt pocket aces; you went all in and some idiot with a jack-seven suit chose to call. The flop came and look what we have – two jacks and a seven. You flopped a nuts straight and you want as much cash as possible. Next comes the turn, then the river, and both brought consecutive cards of an identical suit, giving your opponent a backdoor flush. Runner? Aces cracked. Now, there are two scenarios here – you can flip out or you can let it slide. A famous pro player once said that, win or lose, if you can easily forget the last hand you played, you do not have the mindset a pro player needs.

Tilting is as bad as variance and all poker players experience it. It can be triggered by something so small – perhaps an irritating opponent, a bad call or missing a substantial pot because you laid a huge hand for the sake of caution, even winning a large amount of chips can cause a tilt. Be ready for it because it will happen.

Shift Gears

When it comes to addressing a tilt, the best advice I can give you is to learn how and when to shift gear. To be fair, you should learn how to do this anyway, not wait for a tilt and gear shifting is one of the best and oldest tricks in a pro player's bag. You need to learn when aggression is the right course and when you are conservative. You can learn this by watching what happens at the table. Have you a player or two that are wild? Are there any conservative players – you will know them instantly! When you've played a few thousand hands, you will be able to learn how to shift gears because you will be able to get a feel for the table dynamics, how your opponents play and how they act with each hand.

Is it really worth it – The Time Element

This secret has two tiers to it – the race to win the hand and timing. There is something very distinct that separates the pros from the amateurs. You will note if you observe enough, that a pro player doesn't run after a draw if the odds don't fall in their favor. Let's say you have odds of 3-1 on winning a straight draw but the implied odds are small. A pro will fold a straight draw to any bet made by an opponent. They will wait for better odds and a better opportunity before taking a chance of commitment to a marginal play.

Let's see if I can make that a bit clearer using another, non-poker example. You are investing, for the first time, in a sports business. You have to consider a number of things first – do you have the startup capital needed to build the business? Is the business location easy to get to? What is your niche? Who are your target audience? And, perhaps the most important of all, are you willing to give up all your energy and time to focus on your business investment? Every decision you make comes with a corresponding cost. When you make a choice to do one thing you have to give up something else. In the study of economics, this is known as opportunity cost. If you choose to go with B, you have given up A, C and D. The same principle applies to poker – if you opt to play a marginal hand, and lose it, you are sacrificing the opportunity to win a much bigger hand in the next betting round. The key here is productivity, making and getting the most out of every play you make.

Let's look at another example; studies show that it doesn't matter how cuddly your dog is, it really isn't a good idea to try and stroke its eating! So, when is the best time to pet your dog? Clearly not at mealtimes otherwise you run the risk of being bitten. This may seem like a daft example but it does have a lot of value, especially when it comes to poker. It all comes down to timing. Ask yourself one question – is worth the time, effort and money to be involved in the hand? Is it the right time to engage or should I hold back? Keep these questions in your mind with every hand and you won't go too far wrong.

Safety First

On the night, you have one strategy – to wait for those pocket monsters, the kings and the aces. Playing it safe is the name of the game. Keep this in mind – if you don't put it in the middle, you can't lose it. It's all about getting the recipe right – of how to be careful. Unfortunately, it is also a recipe for losing, or at least only winning small amounts, and of not taking any chances and, at the end of the day, poker is all about chances. It's about making calculated moves. I don't suggest for one minute that you take blind leaps of faith and risk all that you have on a hand that could only be described as marginal. It isn't as painful as being caught by tilt or variance but it won't do your bankroll any favors that are for sure. Play it safe, but not too safe!

Walk that Narrow Path

I want to tell you a story about a boy who left his home in a small town in the Philippines when he was only a teen. He got on a ship and followed his dream of becoming a top boxer, leaving his family behind hm. When he was 16, he won his very first fight, via a unanimous decision. The boy was poor and hungry, he was a target for beatings and he knew just one way to survive – by using his fists. His biggest secret, the one that kept him going and pushed him from his rags to untold riches, was to keep on throwing the punches.

Now, you might ask what this has to do with poker so let me tell you another story. An accountant won a satellite tournament online and got the chance to play in the World Series 203. He beat a pro player, was declared champion, and went on to start a company of his own, using poker sponsorship money to travel. These two stories are so different from each other but both tell the same story about characters and standards. Both men fought to be in the position they are today and both walked a very narrow path, suffering losses and defeats along the way. In fact, some of those losses were devastating but they both soldiered on, giving it all they had and improving to become the best in the world at what they do.

The moral here is to learn to keep your head held high, your standards high and learn when to say yes and no to yourself, all the while moving forward. Many people rush in blindly and then drift, letting the winds of change blow them about. Poker is a game that teaches you planning skills, how to chase your dream aggressively. In fat, regardless of those who say it is just a game; poker is an excellent game for teaching you about life. It teaches you real life lessons, lessons that many take for granted. Learn to be aggressive yet cautious. Think before you act, weigh up your options and prepare, plan and commit. Everything that you should be doing in real life anyway.

Ian Dunross

Chapter 10

Let's Talk Poker – Common Terms Explained

If you are going to learn to dominate your opponents in a game of poker then you must at least know what you are talking about. So many players don't take the time out to learn the terms associated with poker and really don't have a clue what is being talked about in conversation. Poker contains a number of words and saying that sound somewhat like gobbledygook to outsiders and you could be forgiven for thinking that the people talking are under the influence of something other than normal tobacco or alcohol! There are a few sayings that need no explanation, such as:

- Hold your cards close to your chest
- Poker face
- Call your bluff
- I'd rather be lucky than good.

You may already have an understanding of some poker terms and sayings but, particularly for beginners, there are bound to be a lot that are meaningless to you, that you don't understand and may never even have heard – yet. Over the years, the game has gained a number of unique phrases and words, all of which are used in regular conversation by poker players, kind of like their own language. It can be pretty incomprehensible to the untrained ear. After all, as a new player, with little or no knowledge of these words, what would this sound like to you?

"I had pocket rockets and the flop comes Ace, two rags, rainbow giving me top set. Can you believe that donkey, Harry, goes runner, runner and cracks my set with his 23-to-1 shot flush draw? It's just like him; he's such a calling station"

If you understand that completely and can translate it then you have no need to go any further in this chapter! However, if it looks like a foreign language then you need to keep reading. By the end of this chapter, you will be conversant in poker speak and will understand this conversation!

Glossary of Poker Terms

Let's begin with the terms that you most definitely need to familiarize yourself with. Afterwards, we'll go back to that conversation and see if we can't translate it into something more understandable – after all, it is the kind of thing you will hear from others in the world of poker.

All-in

If you put all of your chips in the pot, you are all-in. You cannot participate in any more bets that are over and above your all-in amount. After that, a side-pot will be created for the remaining players and you would only be eligible to share in or take the main pot, not the side pot.

Ante

This is a small bet, forced and set by the house that all players have to post before the deal is made. The ante is used in Stud Poker while in Hold 'Em, blinds are used. Antes also tend to be commonly used in tournaments as well as blinds.

Back Door

A backdoor hand requires that you use both the river card and the turn card to make up your hand. An example of this would be if you are holding a three flush, after the flop, and you need another two cards of the same suit. This is also known as runner.

Bad Beat

This is a good hand that is beaten or cracked by a better one that came from way behind, hitting a lucky draw to move in front. All poker players have at least one bad beat story to talk of.

Big Slick

If you are holding an ace and king in your hand, it is known as a big slick.

Blinds

These are the mandatory bets that are made by players one and two on the left of the dealer button and are called the big blind and the small blind.

Bluff

Betting without a good hand and hoping that your opponent will fall for it and fold, giving you the pot.

Calling Station

This is a derogatory term for a person, who constantly calls, without the right pot odds and, because of it, often win with long shot hands, causing frustration amongst other players. It is also very difficult to bluff a calling station!

Cards Speak

This is when all players turn their cards face up, without a declaration, and the best hand is determined by the cards held – the cards speak for themselves.

Check Raise

You check on your turn for the bet and then, when the next player also bets, you then raise their bet.

Donkey

An opponent who is not a good player and looks as though he or she is just throwing good money after bad. Used to be called a sucker, fish or pigeon.

Double Belly Buster

A hand that has two inside straight draws – for example, a hand with a 7, 9, 10, J, K can be a straight if an 8 or Q turns up. The hand has 8 outs; the same as an open-ended straight draw but is more deceptive because of the double belly buster.

Drawing Dead

A draw that, no matter what card is dealt to you or turns up, you cannot win. Let's say you have four spades one of which is the Ace. You want a spade on the river to give you a King high flush. If the spade appears, you lose to an Ace high flush and, because your opponent has two Aces, you can't win and are drawing dead.

Fish

See donkey – a player who is playing poor and throwing money away

Flop

When the first betting round is over, a series of three cards are dealt, community cards, and these are called the flop

Gunshot

An inside straight draw that only has 4 outs. If you draw to a Q, J, 9, 8, you would need one of the tens to complete a straight

Heads-up

Playing against just one opponent.

Implied Odds

An extension of the pot odds and is the ration of what you could expect to win, should you complete your hand to the total you need to call to carry on. Pot odds are an exact calculation; implied odds are more guesswork and are based partly on the tendencies of your opponents.

Inside Straight Draw

See gut shot.

Isolate

Making a raise with the sole intention of forcing your opponents to fold so that you can play heads up against one opponent, thus isolating him or her.

Limp

Flat calling the big blind amount is to limp into a hand

Monster

An extremely strong hand that is, in all likelihood, a sure winner

Muck

Another word for folding. The dead cards on the table are called the muck.

Nuts

Based on what is on the board, the nuts are the best hand available. A hand that s unbeatable is sometimes called a "lock" or the "Brazils".

Out

This is a card that helps your hand, improving it to make it a winner. Let's say you hold the Ace and nine of hearts and the flop has two hearts. That means you have nine outs to the nut flush because there are nine more hearts in the deck.

Pocket Rockets

If you are playing Hold 'Em, this is a pair of aces

Pot Odds

A ratio worked out from the amount of money in the pot compared to the amount it will take call on the current bet. Say the pot has $100 in it and it costs you $20 to call it, the pot odds are 5 to 1.

Quads

A nickname for four of a kind

Rags

A worthless card, normally small board cards

Rainbow

Three or four board cards that are of different suits. A flop is called a rainbow if it holds three different suits. If the turn card is the fourth suit, a flush is not possible

River

The final community card that is dealt, the fifth one

Runner-Runner

A hand made with the river and the turn cards. Two running cards are called runner-runner. For example, if you had a three flush already and the turn and the river card are the same suit as you're flush, that is called runner-runner.

Sandbag

Playing slow early in the game to hide how strong your hand is. The idea of this is to make more money later on, a deceptive ploy in order to gain profit.

Set

If you have a pocket pair and another one of the rank hit the board that is a set.

String Bet

An illegal move made when a player doesn't voice his intention to raise but puts the chips out to call and then gets more chips to raise.

Tilt

A player who no longer has any discipline and is playing aggressive and loose in a desperate bid to win the pot is said to be on the tilt. This is usually caused by a number of factors including a series of bad beats that cause frustration.

Trips

Different from a set, trips are when there is two of the same rank on the board and you have a third in your hand. It is different from a set because only one player can hold those three to a set while two can hold the same trips when two are on the board.

Turn

This is the fourth community card, dealt out in between the flop and the river card.

Under the Gun

The player immediately to the left of the dealer button who is first to act is under the gun.

Wheel

The smallest straight that consists of Ace-2-3-4-5. Sometimes called a bike or bicycle wheel as well.

Ian Dunross

Poker Speak – Part 2

Now that you have learnt all those wonderful terms, covering all sorts of different definitions in poker, do you now understand the conversation that we used as an example at the beginning of this chapter? In case you missed out something or still don't fully understand, let's run over it again. The unique phrases or words are highlighted in the paragraph below:

*"I had **pocket rockets** and the **flop** comes Ace, **two rags, rainbow** giving me **top set.** Can you believe that **donkey,** Harry, goes **runner, runner** and **cracks** my **set** with his **23-to-1 shot flush draw?** It's just like him; he's such a **calling station."***

Now that same paragraph translated:

*"I had **two Aces in the hole** and the **three cards the dealer dealt** come Ace, **two small cards with three different suits** giving me the **best/highest three of a kind.** Can you believe that **unskilled, bad player,** Harry, he hit two of his needed suit in a row, one*

98

*on the turn and the other on the river and **beats my three of a kind with his long shot flush draw?** It's just like him, **he's a weak player who calls way too much and sometimes gets lucky.**"*

Now you can see just how concise poker speak really is! I guarantee you that it won't be long before you are talking in this way naturally.

Ian Dunross

Chapter 11

The Reasons for Betting in Poker

One of the most fundamental skills in poker, and one you must learn if you want to dominate your opponents, understands the betting. If you want to become skilled, you need to understand why you are betting and how best to manipulate the other players into playing the way you want them to play, so that you can win as many time as possible. Skilled players always know why they are betting and what they want to accomplish from that bet.

This chapter aims to look at the basic concepts for pre-flop scenarios in a no limit Hold 'Em game, when the pot is unopened – these are situations that do not involve you facing a raise.

First you must be aware that, in most poker games, there will be many more reasons to fold that there are to bet or to raise. Because of this, it is vital that you learn how to select a good starting hand. In simple terms, it means that you shouldn't play too many hands – most players do and it is most likely the single biggest reason for failure at the table. It matters not whether you are in a casino or playing online, all of your opponents are there for the same reasons as you – because they love poker and they want to make some money. They are there to play, not to throw their hands away because they can't justify the bet on them. Unless you are experiencing a rare run of very good hands, most times you will be able to throw your starting hand away and not regret it – and save you some money as well.

Why You Should Raise

No doubt you have asked yourself the following question – "why do I need to raise, I only want to see the flop and then see what happens?" You are not the only one, countless other players before you have asked the same question. That is why it is important to understand that this is a losing philosophy and, perhaps more importantly, why it is. While this is not as common or indeed anywhere near as significant as calling when you really should have folded, not raising when you should have will cost you in the long term.

You should be working towards playing an aggressive form of poker and this means that, if you are in the hand, more often than not you will be raising or re-raising. Top reasons for raising are:

1. Thin out the players
2. Take full control of a hand
3. For value
4. To prompt others to fold

Let's look at these reasons in a bit more detail:

Thin out the players

You really don't want to be playing a raised pot when there are more than two opponents in the game. You may have a bog hand but it is still vulnerable to being beaten and you really don't want an opponent to pick up a random two pair or a mad straight draw. The less people left in the game the less people there are to fight against for the pot and that means there are fewer decisions to make. When you enter the hand, you should be looking to raise.

Take full control of a hand

Another excellent reason or raising is that it tells the rest of the players that you have a very good, strong hand. You might miss the flop but you can carry on with the aggressive play with a continuation bet and take the pot down. As you raised pre-flop. The other players are more likely to pay some respect to your next bet. If you do raise pre-flop, more often than not, you will get players who check you after the flop, just so they can see what your intentions are. You now have full control of that hand.

For value

This is really the most common reason for raising, the straightest forward, especially when you have a good starting hand. You might look at your hand and believe that you have best one and want to see more money in the pot – simple, yes? Maybe not. There are other things you need to take into consideration. A pre-flop raise may be a little tricky in terms of the size of the bet because there are several things you want to achieve:

1. More money in the pot
2. To narrow the field down a little

3. You want your opponents to draw badly

You must think very carefully about the size of the bet you need to place in order to meet those three objectives. A recommendation here is to raise three times the blind size plus one additional bet for each limper than is before you. Do that consistently and nobody will be able to read the way you are playing and, on top of that, you should accomplish all of your objectives.

While you are still a beginner, you must keep in your mind that you shouldn't raise the minimum. That is a common mistake – raising the minimum with a pocket pair of aces when a few players have already limped into the hand. This is not a good move because, although aces are the best pre-flop hand, it is highly unlikely that your opponents are going to fold. While you might think you want them to call and build up the pot, in reality, you don't. Aces are not a good hand to win against four other random hands. The point I'm trying to make is that you should raise by an amount that will maximize how much you can win.

To prompt others to fold

Bluffing is a big part of poker but, on occasion, you will be better off if you bet to try and force your opponents to fold, even if they have better hands than you This is very true of tournaments where you to build up your chip stack by stealing blinds and antes. If you are aiming to force your opponents to fold, you must be an aggressive player. A small raise may look like you have a big hand but it may not be enough – bet sufficient to make it so your opponent can't call. However, do keep in mind that each and every bet tells a story of its own. While the most you can do is go all-in if you make it look as you are looking for a fold, you might just get a call from a player who didn't fall for your bluff.

When the Option to Call is there

While you should really be aiming for an aggressive style, especially in No Limit Hold 'Em, there will be times when the best course of action is to call pre-flop, for example:

1. When you are first to act
2. When you can call after other limpers

On occasion, the position you hold at the table, how strong your hand is and a number of other factors will dictate that it is best to limp in and being the first to act is one time when that holds true. However there is one important concept that you must remember – only limp in if you have a hand that you can call a raise with. An example of this would be if you had a small pocket pair that you hope to catches a set with.

If you get into a situation where a number of players have already limped in, you can call but only with certain types of hand – do use good hand selection though. Just because everyone else is playing, it doesn't mean that you can justify playing with any to cards.

While you are learning, if you are faced with a tough decision to make, remember that calling is pretty much the last choice to make. If you have learnt your lessons well, you will be folding more than raising, and raising more than calling. If you call too often with weak hands, you are pretty much on a one-way ticket ride to losing your bankroll.

Ian Dunross

Chapter 12
Proper Bet Sizing

It's one thing understanding the reasons why you are betting but quite another to understand how to size your bets correctly to manipulate and influence what is going on and that know-how is just one of the things that separates an amateur poker player from a pro. Without any doubt, not sizing bets properly is one of the biggest mistakes made by beginners and are a giveaway sign of a lack of experience. Beginner poker players will often bet or raise to the extreme – either too much or not enough.

When you play poker, it is vital that you consider the result of your actions what you want to happen, before you make your bet. You already know why you should bet, now you need to know how much and, for this chapter we are going to look at basic sizing both pre and after the flop.

Bet Sizing before the Flop

One good tip that all beginners should keep in mind is this – raise three times the amount of the big blind, plus one more big blind for each limper that is in the pot. If the hand folds to you, raising by that much is sufficient to make sure that there are not too many players on the field. For example, if you used that tip in a cash game that has blinds of $0.25/$0.50, you would raise by $1.50 - $0.50 x three – but if there were two callers, you would make it $2.50 - $0.50 x three and $0.50 for each of the limpers.

Beginner poker players often make one mistake – raising by the same amount no matter how many players are in the pot. It is, without a doubt, easier to play a game of poker against fewer opponents and, if you don't raise your bet size when there are limpers involved, you are asking for a lot of trouble after the flop.

The three x + 1 formula have been the pre flop standard for many years and it is favored by the vast majority of pro players. That said, it is just as common to see a raise of 2.5 x

+ 1. An example of that would be in a tournament that has blinds of $300/$600. The standard opening raise would be $1500 and not $1800, as you would get with the three x. A lot of players are turning to the 2.5 x formula because they believe the end result will be the same and you are asking far fewer chips. It is also becoming more common to see pre-flop bets mixed up, based on stack size or what stage the tournament is at. For example, a player might start off with the three-x formula but move 2.5 x later on in the tournament.

Betting Too Much

Many beginners are guilty of betting too little pre-flop but another mistake is betting too much. For example, raising five or 6 times the blinds when you are first to act in a game where three x is the standard. OK, so all the players may fold and you could end up picking up the blinds, which, if that was your intention, worked. But, if your intention were to maximize the amount you could win, especially with a good starting hand, you would fail, purely because your bet size was not right.

Adjusting Your Bets

Make sure your bets are based on what you observe of the other players tendencies and other situational factors. If you are in a game where the standard three x or 2.5 x doesn't accomplish what you want to achieve, adjust your bet size accordingly. All games are different and one rule may not work for all games. You may well be in a game where the only way you can accomplish those goals is to raise four or six x the blind. Judge the game you are in when you are calculating the bet size.

Bet Sizing after the Flop

Incorrect bet sizing also happens after the flop. Your bet size has to depend on a number of factors, including the situation of the game. However, a rule of thumb is to size your bet between half the pot and the total of the pot. This will normally mean that draws are given the wrong odds to call, will get worse hands to call and may get better hands for folding.

You must always relate the size of a post flop bet to the size of the pot. For example, if you are in a no limit game and there is $20 in the pot after the flop, a good-sized bet would be $15. But, on the next round, the pot may well be smaller, say $12. If you are staying with the same bet size then your bet should be, based on the size of the pot, $9. This is assuming that you are basing your bet on three quarters of the pot size.

So, what about when it comes to betting the turn? If you bet the flop and are then called, the pot size will be bigger. You have a number of different options for betting on the turn but, if you opt to place another bet, it should be based on the amount of money in the pot. This means that, if you bet on the turn, your bet size will be higher than the flop. Many beginner players do not adjust their bet size to take the pot amount into account – don't make this mistake or it could cost you dearly.

Giving Draws the Incorrect Odds

There will be times, after the flop, where you are playing against someone who is holding a drawing hand. One key component of a successful poker game is to charge your opponents for the chance to draw out on you. If you are playing a fixed limit game, you can only go as far as the betting limits allow for but in no limit games, you can size your bet so that the cost of them drawing goes above and beyond their chances of completing a flush or a straight.

The following are a few typical amounts to bet that are relative the size of the pot and the odds offered up to your opponents:

1. Bet ¼ of the pot amount and give your opponents 5-1 odds

2. Bet ½ of the pot amount and give your opponents 3-1 odds

3. Bet ¾ of the pot amount and give your opponents 2.33-1 odds

4. Bet the full amount of the pot and give your opponents 2-1 odds

If you only bet ¼ of the pot amount, you will be giving your opponents decent odds for drawing. But a bet of ¾ of the pot amount, against just one opponent, would be sufficient to rule out any common draws. Even if that opponent falls lucky, he or she will lose in the long run when the odds offered by the payoff are shorter than those he or she is drawing to now.

As a rule, it is usually better to bet more than less but don't get caught in a common trap – betting just to protect the hand you have. In poker, you should be betting to maximize the amount you could possibly win while minimizing what you could lose. If you make sure your bet is structured so that the pot offers evens on a call but offers odds against the other player making their hand, you will win in the long run.

Varied against Consistent Bet Sizes

Always remember that your bet tells your opponents a story so do try not to fall into a pattern, either pre or post flop. One of the more common patterns for amateur players is to raise their bet on a strong hand and lower it on weak hand and this will very easily become predictable. Once that happens, more experienced opponents will exploit that predictability, costing you big time.

To prevent yourself from becoming too readable, there are two things you can do. Vary your bet size randomly or stick to the same bet increment every single time. You would vary your bet sizes if you wanted to throw your opponent off the scent and keep them on their toes guessing at the time. On the other hand, if you keep your bet size consistent, no matter whether you are bluffing or you have a good hand or not, your opponents will find your bluffs more believable and will not be able to discern any patterns. A general guideline to follow for beginners would be to bet consistently. Always raise by three x + 1 for each limper and always size your bet to ¾ of the pot amount after the flop and nobody will be able to read any stories in your game.

Chapter 13

Playing Marginal Poker Hands

It used to be that the phrase "marginal hands" was frowned upon, especially for new players who were trying to learn the game. Indeed, new players were advised to avoid these hands at all costs. The first important rule an amateur learned was not to lay too many hands and the second rule was to become familiar with starting hands so that they could understand how the hand values related to position. Putting these two rules together formed one mantra – *"**Play only quality holdings and play them aggressively"**.*

While this is rather a simple piece of advice, it remains the same advice today to keep the newer players from falling into trouble.

That said, to stop your opponents from becoming a little too familiar with the way you play, you should mix things up a bit. Predictability does not win poker hands so you need to be able to play different hands in the same ways. If you don't, your opponents will know what kind of hand you have simply by the amount you bet or raise. To throw them off the scent throw in a few non-premium hands and play them the same way you would a strong hand, just to add a little disguise to your game.

Marginal Hands Can Have Potential

Marginal poker hands are not standard; they can come in all shapes and sizes. The one thing they are is good drawing hands, consisting of suited cards, connectors, and small pairs and gapped cards. These are all hands that won't win without some improvement but they do have potential. This is because no limit games are game of implied odds and a marginal hand has the potential to become a monster hand – if it is played properly, your marginal hand can sweep all of your opponents chips away from them in one go.

There is a vast difference between a marginal hand and a junk hand. Marginals can become strong hands while junk hands need your opponents to abandon if you are going to take the pot with them. Most of the time, junk hands are played out of the big blind for free and if you find that you are playing a junk hand on another position, you have gone a little too far.

The Management of Deception

The biggest cornerstone of winning a game of Hold 'Em is making sure that you play a good solid hand from the right position. If you want to maximize the amount you can win on a good hand, you must give the table the illusion of action. Much of the game of Poker revolves around deception and playing a marginal hand from a late position or, if appropriate, from an earlier position, will give you the illusion you want to achieve at little cost to you, while also giving you the potential to connect to a big hand and make a large sum of money.

Showing down a marginal starting hand every now and again will increase your ability to get the action on your strong hands. However, don't do this too often because it will very easily work against you and will run your bankroll down instead of increasing it.

Outplaying Your Opponents

If you stick to playing just the good cards, then you will be playing nothing more than ABC poker and praying that your hands are better than your opponents are. You know, deep down that, in the long run, that really isn't going to happen so unless you are resigned to breaking even, you need to give some serious thought to how you are going to outplay your opponents and win these pots without the aid of good hands. How do you do that? The first way would be to look for situations that are profitable to play marginal holdings. There are two elements that you need to consider here – your position and their style of playing. One other element that you should know about is this – and this is a real note of caution. If you win by your wiles alone, it will soon become very heady and intoxicating – so much so that you could end up on a very slippery slope of overplaying the tactic without the backup of good cards. I don't think I need to go into too much detail about what will happen when your opponents realize just how you have been winning all along. Suffice it to say, it won't be pretty! Be cautious, pick your spots and combine knowledge of your adversaries with position and you will be just fine.

Of course, there is a caveat to this – If you play against losing players on a regular basis, players that don't pay any attention to the way you play, you don't need to mix up your play to confuse them. They are not thinking about what you might be holding in your hand so stick to the ABC poker and exploit their weak play rather than wasting fancy play on them. Just remember that a good chunk of the money you win at poker doesn't come from you paying a cracking hand; it comes from the ineptitude of your opponents.

From Marginal Hands to Junk Hands

Do yourself a favor and don't start falling in love with starting hands. They change value quite frequently as the game progresses and not always for the best. Let's take a look at a hand that is classed as marginal and well worth playing but loses some of the shine as the game progresses:

You are holding and eight and nine hearts in the middle position. Two players have limped in and the next one raises by the minimum. You feel a little lucky with this hand so you call, and so do the first two that limped in. The flop has nailed your cards, giving you a straight with a ten clubs, jack diamonds and queen spades. You were going for a flush draw but that has gone out of the window – a straight on the flop isn't a bad hand though. So, next, the first limper bets half the pot and the second one call. The original player to raise now re-raises.

That has stopped you in your tracks because, all of a sudden, you come to realize that you are actually holding on to a sucker straight, the idiot end and you might just be in some trouble here. You had two suited connectors that could have been a good marginal hand and it all just turned to junk. Do try not to get in too deep when you are holding on to the bottom end of the straight – many good players have lost their stack over that.

Domination

Your biggest losers over the long term will be marginal hands that can be dominated very easily, especially if you don't know how to get away from them. If you have, let's say a suited Ace rag and you opt to enter into the game with it, remember the reasons why you played the hand in the first place. With this hand, your goal should be to try to get a cheap flop while trying to get a flush. Don't get too excited if an ace drops on the flop, someone may be holding a better one.

An ace, jack hand is also marginal because it is easily dominated. The same is true of a hand like king, queen, jack, king, and ten. There is some very good poker advice that you should keep in mind – when in doubt, get out. That can save you a lot of heartache and whole bunch of chips as well. Instead of looking at these marginal hands as ones that you can play, think about how enjoyable it is to see others playing those same kinds of hands against your ace, king hand.

Yes, you may flop a spectacular hand with a marginal but the hard truth is that the best hands going in and the best ones coming out. If you start off second best, it is very easy to fool yourself into sticking with it if it looks like staying that way. Avoiding your hand being dominated is the best way to preserve your bankroll and, after all, the object of your game is to dominate others, not the other way around.

Ian Dunross

Chapter 14

General Strategy Tips for Online Cash Poker

The tips I am going to give you in this section are aimed at improving your online game play but you can also use these for live poker games. First, I want to discuss why you should always opt for no limit when you are playing Hold 'em poker games. Then I will move on to tips that are more specific, covering specialized strategies that are suitable for new players and that some advanced players can also take note of.

Why No Limit Hold 'Em?

You may be one of those players that plays limit games only or a mix of limit and no limit so you might be interested in why I say that you should opt for no limit games more often than limit games. There is an old saying that says that no limit games are "the Cadillac of Poker" but the main reason is that, in a no limit game, a bad player, or a fish as they are termed, will pay a far higher price for the mistakes they make than they would when they play in limit games. That is the main reason and I want to refer you to the following, which comes from Sklansky's Theory of Poker. This is his fundamental theorem of poker:

'Every time a player plays differently than he would play if his opponents hole cards lay open then he makes a mistake and loses; on the contrary, every time a player plays the same way as he would play if his opponents hole cards lay open, he would make no mistake and he'd gain.'

This is, quite simple, the ground rule for playing poker, no matter what type, as it highlights the main borderline that separates a good player from a bad one. A player who can read another player and the cards will make far fewer mistakes than one who is bad at it.

Now, let's assume that we have bad player who is constantly making mistakes; playing Limit Hold 'Em would see him lose over the long term but, as there is a limit on the betting stakes, he won't lose quite so much as he would in a No Limit game. If your fish player has a top pair and you have trips, he is going to think that he is winning. In a 1/2 Limit, you can bet 2 – pre flop and on the flop – or 4 – post flop. You will also be raising and re raising by 2 and 4 respectively. If you played in No Limit, you would be able to re raise all in with your maximum amount for buy in – leaving the fish gasping for air.

Multi-Table Poker and Bonuses

When you go to a new online poker game, stick to playing one table at a time. It is best to get yourself adapted and comfortable with the environment before you start playing on multiple tables – you will make fewer mistakes.

When you go to online poker games for the first time, sign up at a few places that offer sign up bonuses first. Try a few rooms out before you pick on one and play it long term. A word of caution first though, where sign up bonuses are concerned. You may get the feeling that you can play just to clear the bonus.

Do try to avoid thinking like that, not only because it makes you think that you should be playing extremely efficiently (although that is never a bad thing; you can also lose any joy you have for the game. There are many players who clear their bonus amount extremely quickly, playing on multiple tables and spending all their time to see how many raked hands they can play.

This will not only ensure you lose your enjoyment; it will also make you play worse. If you spend your time playing on multiple tables and clearing your bonuses you will be manly lying a tight card game instead of playing a people game, which is what you should be doing. This means that you are not watching what your opponents are doing and are focused only on your own game. And, even if you use one of any number of poker tools available, trying to watch hundreds of different stats at multiple tables at the same time is simply not realistic, nor is it an effective use of your time or skills.

Play WITH the bonuses but never play FOR the bonuses. Treat a sign up bonus, or any other bonus, as an added extra and never play with more tables than you should. Think of it this way – most of your winnings are going to come from bad players, not from those bonuses

Now, although I have said you should play one table only, there is a large argument in favor of playing those multiple tables, apart from being more efficient at clearing bonuses. DISCIPLINE. It can get boring if you only play one table at a time especially if you are on a bad run. Sometimes you might have to fold 30 or 40 hands in arrow and even the best of players get bored with that! Multiple tables can help you to overcome the boredom factor but don't overdo it.

Position

The very best tip I can give you for cash games is to learn hand rankings before you start to play. It's no good not knowing what you have in your hand or not knowing what it means in terms of the game.

Try, if you can, to sit right of a tight player and left of one who is aggressive. If you sit to the right of the tight player and raise, he will move out of the pot most likely, giving you a chance to pick up a larger pot. It will also help you to be able to steal more blinds. Sitting at the left of an aggressive player is even more vital. First, it makes you tighter and more disciplined and, second, if you have a real monster you can trap him. Then you can re raise pre flop or, on rare occasions, slow play by calling. You can also raise on the flop. Position is vital, especially when it on an aggressive player.

Make sure that maintain discipline by playing a positional game. This means playing loose on the button and in a late position, rather than early or middle. You will win more than in the long run because you will have the luxury of having information before you have to make your decision – it's best to be last in play.

Steal the button whenever you get the chance, even with a mediocre hand. Position is way more valuable than the cards you hold and this kind of aggression will only serve to irritate players, making them think that you are a loose cannon – this will result in your good hands being called more easily.

If you have lots of opponents in your game, you should still play suited connectors and pocket pairs that are low or middle. These are drawing hands and, when there is a big pot with a lot of players calling, you will still get pot odds. If you have only one to three other players in the game, play your big pairs and high cards only. You don't want any more than two other opponents really too many will decrease your pre-flop advantage.

Never overrate your position. Throw away rubbish hands on the button but still play the low suited connectors or those semi connecters as the button remains. This will give you a good advantage.

Playing Styles

Betting and raising in poker is far better than calling and checking, unless you are deliberately slow playing. Callers are seen as losers in poker and, as such, you should be betting and raising, not just because you may have the best hand or are bluffing but because that's what poker is all bout – making decisions. Aggressive players put their opponents to the decision – it's no good being a passive player, it won't get you anywhere.

Whether you are passive or aggressive has everything to do with the way you bet and the amounts you bet. Being a loose or tight player is all about the number of cards you play pre flop. Passive players should look for aggressive tables to play while aggressive players should look for passive tables to play. A truly good player can play both and will always play opposite to the style of the table.

Poker is all about adapting. If you are playing a tight table, you should be playing loose; if you are playing an aggressive table, you should play passively. If you have a pair of aces under the gun on a table that is aggressive, call - there is a good chance that somebody else will bet behind and you can gain value from your hand.

You will see people who are multi-tabling – you will see the same names listed on a done different tables or someone at your table is playing slow, indicating they could be playing at more than one table. If you come across this n your game, turn up the aggression. They won't want any trouble so will re raise a lot more. If a player suddenly begins playing fast, there is a good chance they have a monster so be prepared to lay a good hand down against them.

Keep an eye on the size of the stack of each of your opponents, especially if you are in tournament play. Don't play risky games against players with bigger stacks than you have; save the risk for those players with lower stacks.

Respect raises and re raises at least 85% of the time, especially if they are made by players who are passive or tight. If you are playing aggressive players, these should be respected at least 65 to 70% of the time. Not many people have the guts needed to re raise a bluff.

Do you want to know how to play a stack/blind ratio? Here's an example. Let's assume that you have $500, your opponent is playing with $25 and the blinds are $2 - $4. You are in the big blind and you have a Jack Ten. Your opponent moves all in from sitting under the gun, or the first position and all the other players at the table fold. Now, in this situation, you should really fold as well because you will need to risk $21 just to try to take his last $25 and that is not profitable play.

If your opponent had $500, the same as you, a call might be an acceptable play because you then have the chance of taking $500 for a $21 risk. Making the decision on whether or not to call depends on how that player is playing after the flop and on how many chips he has.

Another example would be this. Both you and your opponent have $1000 each and the blinds are $2 - $4. You have a pair of queens and make to $20 to go. Your opponent is behind you and moves all-in with $1000. Fold, unless you know for absolute certainty that your opponent is not holding a pair of kings or aces. If the same play were made by an opponent who only had $60, you would call his bet, hoping that he hasn't get that pair of aces or kings.

Try to keep raises down to 70 to 100% most of the time unless you have a monster hand. This will save you money when an opponent calls or re raises you with a stronger hand. If you have limpers ahead of you, try to raise between four and six times the big blind

Only resort to slow playing when you have a hand that is going to hold up and when there are no flushes or straight draws.

If you are playing a fishy game, pull a few tricks from your sleeve when you feel like doing it. For example, if want to project a tight image, just make ¾ raises. If no one calls you, advertise. Show your bad cards and the bad players will assume that you are a bit of a loose maniac. Sit back and wait for those good cards and then repeat the play. Your opponents will call you a lot faster. Please don't try those on medium or high stake players because they will see straight through it!

Play aggressive as much as possible. This won't only help you to pick up pots; it will also help you to pick up a bit of knowledge. Let's say you have a pair of queens and the flop is a king, two eight. You bet, your semi-aggressive opponent raises – don't call because you will have to call him at the turn and the river. Instead, he raises a little. If the player goes over the top, you will know that your hand is beaten; you don't need to call the bests later on down the line and you will save yourself a lot of money.

Sometimes, if raise with a big slick and the flop hits low cards all the way, you should go ahead and bet the flop if you are in the early position and most definitely if you hold a late position and the previous player has checked to you (only if he isn't in the habit of constantly check-raising though). You could also opt to check the hand but this isn't recommended too often. If your flop-represent bet is called, be careful – ask yourself if your cards have helped your opponent.

Do not slow play on a pair of kings or aces – these are not hands to play against a table of more than 2 opponents.

Playing a table of three or four opponents can be a deadly game, even if you hold one of those hands. The same applies to a two pair. Never overrate it because it can be beaten by a flush, straight or full house on the turn and the river when there is a draw. Betting little and often, picking up a decent pot is better than losing it all right at the end.

Be a proactive player, not a reactive one. When you play online, keep your bluffs to a minimum; after all, it only takes one click of the mouse to call. This is never truer than when you are hunting bonuses. Don't make things complicated for you – just play a decent straightforward game of poker. There is time for tricks when you have experience and have proven yourself to be a truly good poker player. That said, you can bluff online, provided you are not playing too many tables and you have a reasonable understanding of your opponents.

Many players play the river wrong. Keep in your head that, after the river card, there are no more cards so slow play is no longer an option. If you have slow played in the early position all through, don't forget you must bet all on the river or your opponent is going to check, leaving you with nothing.

That said if you are not entirely convinced that you have a good winning hand, check most of the time.

Mental Management

Play nice with the fish. Never lose your temper with a fish just because they play badly and made you lose a large pot (combined with luck as well). Instead, compliment a fish on their play; they will then make the same play again in a future game. After all, if you explained where he went wrong, he'd just improve and that is not what you want. Bear in mind as well, that when you first start this is what more experienced players will be doing to you!

There is no way that you win every day, beat each game and win every single pot. It is important that you beat this into your brain. One of the most important parts of learning poker is accepting that fluctuations are all a part of it. Some people will g days or weeks without winning a single game. Bad streaks are even worse when you play cash games online because then you can go on tilt and you do not want this. This can make you change your game because you will start to believe that it is you who is playing badly and playing wrong. When you feel this beginning to happen, stop and take a break away from poker. Leave it a few days, a couple of weeks, however long it takes for you to see that you have your game back and really want to get started again. Don't ever lose your enjoyment of poker because it is your joy that is one of the biggest motivations of paying, apart from the potential winnings of course.

Learn to know when it is time to move on. If the table doesn't feel right or you are not finding it easy to guess your opponents, walk away and go to another table. Never feel bad r ashamed about walking away without making any profit, especially if you are still a beginner. Instead, see it as the right move – if you stayed, you could very well end up losing everything.

Instead of trying to find a reason why you should play a particular hand, look for reasons why you should not play it. This keeps your thought processes stimulated and maintains discipline.

Take some time out every now and again. Poker is a good fun game to play but it can also consume all your mental energy. Go for a walk, have something to eat, anything to give your brain a break and empty it of all poker-related thoughts.

Then you can go and play again. You cannot play your best if you are stressed out or not motivated enough.

If you opt to play high stakes poker, keep in mind that all of the players ahead of you are far better. You can use this to your advantage by always keeping ahead of them. With a low stakes game, your brain should not be processing any more than two steps ahead. This means asking yourself what your opponent thinks you have and what he thinks that you think he has. Play top stakes and you need to be thinking further ahead.

If you play full ring games, play it tight; for shorthand tables, play looser. The more players there are in a game, the tighter you should play and the less there are, the looser you can play. The same is true if you are in a pot. If you have only one opponent they you can play a loose aggressive game but never if there are 6 people in the pot.

Other Tips

When you join a new table, do not ever post your very first big blind before you are the big blind. Poker is all about patience and, if you are not careful, you will lose big money over the long term without even noticing, if you continue posting a blind when you do not need to. The same is true if you come back after sitting out. Do not post dead blinds; be patient and wait for the big blind.

Watch other players and keep notes on habits they may keep or weird stuff they may do. I really can't say this enough to you, especially if you are playing just one or two rooms. It is very important to have a database of other players because it can be the one thing that gives you the edge when you are playing. Every little bit of information is vital, even if it seems stupid. You can note down betting patterns, such as strange all-in bluffs made on the river, time patterns, such as how long a player tends to spend thinking if he has the nuts, and is that an accurate timeframe.

This sort of information cannot be gained by using a poker tool so do the work yourself. Making notes about players also tends to keep you focused on them and not just on your cards. If you are to make any money in poker, you must take it seriously and keeping detailed notes puts you on the road to becoming a real expert.

You have been told, more than once, I don't doubt, that suited connectors can be real goldmines in no limit games and this is absolutely true. If you make flushes and straights they will, more often than not, be the nuts. BUT, do not play any suited connecters that are lower than 7/8 – lower connecters tend to lose on big pots.

Be careful about when you play online cash games. Scientific research has shown, beyond a doubt, that after a dinner break and on the weekends in Europe, you will find the biggest number of players. Monday to Friday, during normal working horse you are likely to come across the pro players, those who play poker 24/7. Early morning or late night Saturday and Sunday are also good times to play in European games – many people head out of the pub a little worse for wear at those times and head to the computer to play – usually playing maniac games.

One last tip – when you are making buddy lists, be sure not to add just a fish – make sure you add the real fishiest of all of the fishes, the real bad players who don't know their hands, and don't know that a pair is lower than a flush. Otherwise, your buddy list will be full of people and that is not what it is all about. The idea of the buddy list is to extract the worst players from the fishpond.

Ian Dunross

Chapter 15

How to Truly Dominate the Poker Table

Have you ever found yourself in the position of losing a large pot simply because you were holding a straight or flush draw and couldn't catch the card that you needed to complete it? Believe it or not, it has happened to every player and it isn't a good feeling. Because, as you well know, when you are on a draw you are only one card away from taking all those chips and adding them to your stack. You just want to keep calling because; eventually your card will appear, on the turn or on the river.

What actually ends up happening is that you have to pile loads of chips in just so that you can call all those bets. That makes you committed to that pot and if you don't catch the card, you are well and truly screwed.

What if there was a way to ensure that all other players checked around when you were on the draw? A way to make sure you didn't have to risk your chips and would only need to bet once you knew if you had caught the card you wanted? And, even better, what if there was a way to win the hand without catching your card?

Luckily, there is such a technique in which you can make it all happen. Want to know how? Read on...

Put yourself in this situation – you are sixth to act on an eight player no limit table. You get a five and a six of diamonds dealt you. Pete and Paul both call and now it's on you.

Suited connectors are great, aren't they, especially when you can bust out your opponents unexpectedly so get in there and call.

The players that are behind you muck their cards straight away because they are frightened off by all the action.

The flop hits with a four diamonds, nine spades and seven diamonds.

What does that mean? It means that you have just flopped an open-ended straight flush draw – what better flop could there be in this situation?

Unfortunately, out comes Bill, firing on all cylinders with a $20 bet – no hesitation

This time Pete and Paul fold and the action is to you

Now you are going to put Bill on a high pocket pair, or you could maybe go Ace nine or Ace seven. He is now thinking that the cards on the board didn't really do anyone any good, hence the reason for the strong bet.

That puts you in something of a tough place....

Think about this one – if you call, you could miss the straight or flush draw on the turn. If you do that, Bill will put another strong bet in and then what will you do?

If, on the other hand, you call to see the river and miss it, you will have handed Bill your chips and lost what was a major hand.

But, you don't want to fold because you have a handful of outs and you really want to win!

So, what would you do if you found yourself in this situation?

Many beginners do not think ahead and they would call Bills $20 bet. If they missed on the turn, they would then call another bet to see the river.

And if they miss the river, they would most likely fold and watch Bill take their chips – and then they would be asking themselves why they never seem to catch the right cards.

An experienced player would have anticipated what was going to happen and would call to see the turn – folding if Bill bet again.

And then there are the tight players who wouldn't even have dreamed of playing the original deal of five and six of diamonds in the first place.

So, what do you do?

Remember, you have that five and six of diamonds. The board says four diamonds, nine spades, and seven diamonds. Bill, who already made a very strong pre flop raise, has just bet $20 after the flop.

The answer?

You RAISE.

Not a silly little raise either, go another $40 to play.

Most players wouldn't even consider raising in this situation but, by doing so, here is what you have done:

1. You have taken control of the hand and you have just bought yourself a freebie card, right when it counts. You see - if Bill were to call that $40 raise, when the turn hits he is going to check on you. That means that you see the turn and the river for $40 more – a real bargain when you think what Bills next bet may have cost you

2. You are representing possible trips. Bill now has to be wondering if you called his pre-flop raise with nothing more than a low pocket pair and were lucky enough to catch the trips on the flop. Or, you may well have a

high pocket par and the raise simply hasn't phased you

3. You have raised the stakes in your favor. Not his. If you had just called his bets and hit the eight diamonds on the turn, what would have happened? Bill would have seen the three diamonds and will have cottoned on to the possibility of a straight and that means he likely won't make any more large bets and he won't call any large bets from you. By doing what you have done, you have raised the stakes by $40, thus increasing your chances of a much bigger pot than if you had done nothing more than called. Does that make sense?

4. Last, but by no means least, you have provided yourself with a way of winning even if you don't catch the flush or the straight. You get to see what Bill's reaction is to your $40 raise and, if you see any sign of weakness, you could bluff and buy the pot if you can't catch the flush or the straight. If you had only called the bet all the way, he wouldn't fall for the bluff but raising $40 is guaranteed to get his brain ticking over.

Now, back to the hand

Bill will shuffle chips around for a minute or two, look at his cards, thinking. He is holding an ace and a nine so he has a top par with the kicker. It's a good hand but it is not a monster, not by a long shot.

Bill calls

The next card is turned and it's a queen spades

No help whatsoever.

Bill checks – that is important

This is your free card that your $40 raise bought you

You are now in complete control of this game so you can check and you can see the river for fee. You still have a lot of outs so you won't lose anything

OR, you could choose to bet strong, trying to scare Bill off. Try pushing $100 in the middle. You may only have a queen high and a beginner player will bet thinking that this is crazy play.

Bill thinks about things for a minute and the mucks it, leaving you to rake in a large bountiful pot.

Even if he had called, you were still holding a good number of outs and, if you had missed, well you could have tried another bluff.

Now, step back in time for a minute to when the flop came out.

After Bill bet the $20, what would have happened if you had opted to call instead of raising?

The queen would still have come out and Bill would straight away have fired off an $80 bet

You would have had two choices – call to see the river or muck your straight flush draw

That explains, I hope, why it is vital that you take complete control of a game of poker. It is this kind of technique that is going to let you dominate the table and win – big.

Chapter 16

The Ten best ways to improve your Poker today!

You have gone over what poker is and all of its different strategies that you could use as a beginner. But there are certain things that you could use to ensure that you increase your knowledge of poker right before your game. This chapter leaves you with the ten simple ways by which you can improve your poker. You can consider these tips as a revision of your game!

Human beings love it if everything they have to do can be done in a shorter way! This chapter helps you do that! You will be able to improve your game this very instant!

You need to know your numbers

There are certain things about poker that you will need to know in order to be a consistent winner. The most important thing is to know and understand he mathematical parameters of poker. Let us assume that you are playing Texas Hold'em. You have decided to put four of your cards down to a flush. You have whether the odds are for or against you completing that hand. If you were in this situation, what would you do?

You may now wonder how you will ever know if the odds against making a certain move, like a fold or a raise, are in your favor or not. You will need to identify the positive expectations of you winning at poker. This is what poker is all about. You will have to identify the situations when you will make a profit and see if you could ensure the situations are on replay!

To know when to associate appositive expectation to a strategy that you use is one of the most important and critical parts of winning at poker. Let us assume that you are faced with having to make a call of 40 into a pot that has $200. You know that the odds of losing are 3 − 1. This is a positive expectation. Assume that this was repeated for 1000 times. This would mean that you would lose $40 seventy five percent of the time. But for every loss, there is that one time you win. You have a twenty five percent chance of winning $200. This leaves you with a sum of $5000. Your net win is what is very important. The number of times you win or lose in a certain hand is not the criteria.

It is a brilliant idea to use the concepts of mathematics and statistics and apply them to poker. You could then find the probability of you winning or losing with ease.

You have to know your opponents

There may have been quite a few times when you would have made the best move in your strategy but would have lost. Why do you think that is the case? This is because you have chosen the wrong opponent to challenge. Have you ever tried to bluff against a person or your opponent who is known to catch bluffs at the very second? This will never work in your favor. It is true that you know this. Everybody knows this. But you and every other player may make this mistake!

If it were only mathematics that you needed to win the game, the players at the top of the winning table would only be the mathematicians. Most often, it is not them! It is always a good thing to know and to understand your opponents. You need to observe your opponents and try to see how they react to situations. Try to understand how it is that they make their choices. Check if there was any particular move that was made that led them to make their decision.

Have you seen them play in every round or hand? Have you seen them raise when they have a hand that is not worth it? Have they always been right? It will not take you more than an hour to understand the players at the table. The right time for any player to watch the other players is when you are not in the hand. If you find that you are waiting for a game, be happy! You have the time to understand and gauge your opponents. You will be able to identify which strategy you will need to use!

Ego, what is that?

This has to be the way that you play the game. Your ego should never cloud your judgment during the game. You would have come across the phrase, 'This is business, not personal' from The Godfather written by Mario Puzo. You should never let yourself be led into the game by your ego. If there is a player who has won the biggest pot from you, you will have to let it go. If he has given you the stink eye or the laugh of a carefree man, ignore it!

When you decide that you have to go by the motto 'Tit for tat', you are only hurting your chances of winning. If you do that, you will only ensure that you lose some more. If you have found yourself losing continuously to the same player, you should just finish his game and leave. You would not want to make a scene. He will feel bad himself if he has to!

You have to keep the records

It is always good to keep your records up to date. How will you know whether or not you are winning or losing otherwise? There are players who have managed to deceive themselves when they have failed to keep a record of their wins and losses. There are quite a few players out there who will have you believe that they are winners for as long as they live. But every person knows that this is not the truth. If you hear someone tell you that they are winners and will always be winners, ask for their records. If you find that he has only recorded his wins and not his losses, you learn that he is a person who has decided to only see what he wants to see. To be honest, this is an illusion!

It is true that it is terribly difficult to record a huge loss! But it is essential that you record this since you will be able to stop you from deceiving yourself. Every human being has a mind that is capable of deceiving itself if it chooses to!

Always choose the best game!

It is true that your strategies play a key role in helping you win. But, it is also true that your winnings often come from the poor play of your opponents. You have to identify your weak opponents. It is always good to choose the weakest opponents for a game. There are players who always call when they have poor hands and fail to raise when they have strong hands. It is always good to play with such people. It is true that you will win a game when there are players who never care about the strength of their hand but call too much.

You need to ensure that you are committed to excellence

Do you have the aim to be the greatest poker player at your table? For this, you will need to commit yourself to greatness. You have to always declare that you are excellent. You can only do this by ensuring that you declare it the day you play! You have to start off with the cards that you have in your hand.

You can use the law of attraction for this! You will need to visualize that you are the greatest poker player there ever was. You will then have to begin acting in the same way. You will find yourself reaching excellence within the beat of your heart. You can do it every single day! If you have decided to be a player who always wins, you will have to ensure that you commit to it. You will find that it is easy to achieve the changes that you choose to make. It is however difficult to maintain those changes. You can always commit to excellence. But, you will need the strongest will power to ensure that you live by it!

You need to practice!

The best way to practice your game and the different strategies that you would want to use is by playing as many hands as you can. But, there is a better way. You could use different software that will help you test your theories and your strategies. It will be like you are playing a real game against a set of poker players. You will find yourself making faster progress. You will become a poker player faster!

There are certain good things about the computer! It can do so much more than a mere human being. Assume that you are trying to test a theory between eight players. You may identify whether or not your theory is foolproof. But, think of all the time you will be wasting. You could take days or weeks or even years before you can obtain a conclusion. But what is the point of this research if you cannot use it? It would only be useful for you if you could play poker in your afterlife. But, you and every other poker player are worried only about how he will do at present. For this, you will need to test your theories faster. Your best friend is your computer!

Make sure you read the groups

You may or may not have a computer. If you do not have a computer, the best thing for you to do would be to go and buy yourself one right now. Once you set up your laptop, connect to the Internet and join the groups that give you all the information that you need about poker. You could join a lot of different groups to understand. You will find yourself facing a lot of talk on these groups. You may find this talk pointless. But, there will be a lot of information on the different strategies that you could use and a lot of interesting facts about poker.

You will never find these ideas anywhere else apart from the group where they were posted. This is not done in order to maintain secrecy. This is because the only people who talk on these groups are very knowledgeable when it comes to poker. Since it is a closed group there are chances that new ideas can be formulated on these websites. The ideas are often posted on the groups and there are a million people who will comment.

Have you ever come across the term 'warp speed'? It is the term used in Star Trek to talk about the speed of the ship. In the same way, the information on these groups is at warp speed! You will find that there are new ideas that have begun to develop. Within the next few hours, you may find that these new ideas have been molded to form better ideas. This molding is done by the best poker players and thinkers. If you are someone who is serious about understanding the game to its fullest, you will need to take part in the conversations held on the Internet. You need to keep up with the trending issues of poker!

Analyze your game and your opponent's game

You have to constantly think when you are either at the table or not. You will have to think even when you are not involved in the particular hand that is being played. You need to watch your opponents constantly. You have to identify the different cards that they are holding. Check if they are the intelligent ones or the silly ones. You have to see which of your opponents is making the best decisions and which opponent the worst. You have to try to see if your opponents bluff too often or if they are bad at bluffing. When you begin to observe them, you will find that there is a pattern in which they use their strategies. You will then have to plan your strategy accordingly. You will never win if you bluff when there is an opponent who is always correct at calling someone.

You will have to think of your strategy too! Based on your records, try to identify the different hands that have led you to success or failure. You have to identify and determine the plays that can be used as an alternative in order to win! There is a thin line between winning and losing at poker. It is your strategies that help to ensure that you do not lose all the time!

You need to concentrate on what matters

There are times when you may begin to concentrate on the wrong things. At such times, the best thing for you to do would be to hope that you get lucky. The dealer would never change the deck even if you wanted him to! You will neither win nor lose. But, why is it that you are concentrating on an aspect that barely matters?

There are a lot of bad beat stories at every poker table! You will listen to all these stories before long. You may lose the game although you had a great hand. But why would you want to waste time pouting about the fact that your opponent has earned some luck? It is true that luck favors every person. That is not the point here. You will need to think about what you could have done better in order to win. That is what matters most!

See what it was about your strategy that made you lose. Try to identify what it was that you could have done differently in order to ensure that you could have won. There is no point in thinking about luck or the deck. There could also be the possibility that you think that the dealer is out to get you. This does not help you in any way. It makes you unproductive. You may want to do this in order to make yourself feel better. It only makes you believe in the lies and not in the reality. You will find it difficult to win!

You will have to face the fact that you will never become an expert in the snap of a finger. It will take time. There are a few shortcuts that you could use along the road to ensure that you become excellent at the game. Some of the examples are software, books, toys, or even computers. If you do not invest in these tools, you will find yourself losing three or four times the money that would have gone into investing in these tools. If you have dreamt that you will become the world's greatest poker player, you will have to work towards the steps that will help you reach that goal.

You need to read all the books

There are quite a few players who grumble about the books. They claim to have played for a number of years and believe that the books do not teach them anything about the game. But, it is these players who have the belief that if the deck of cards was changed; they would win. They may also believe that there is a dealer who has made it his life's mission to harass a poker player. These players have been making this very mistake for the number of years that they have been playing. It is the attitude that they possess that brings them down. They continue to repeat this mindless behavior repeatedly.

There are quite a few good things about the books on poker. It is a good idea to read them! You will get a lot of ideas when you read one book. You need to remember that the books that you buy for poker are not an expense. They are an investment. You will be able to improve your game tremendously.

Ian Dunross

Chapter 17

Typical Beginner Mistakes

By now, you should be more than aware of how to play poker and how to dominate the table. There is still a great deal to learn though. In fact, with poker, you never really stop learning so, before you move on and build on your knowledge, let's review some of the more common mistakes that beginners make – and that you shouldn't make if you want to be the dominator on your table. All of these mistakes are relevant to all forms of Hold'Em Poker, as well as to other formats of the game. Use these mistakes as a guideline so you don't fall into the traps that other beginners do.

So, in no specific order, here are the top 10 typical mistakes made by poker beginners:

Playing too many hands

This is one of the single biggest mistakes made by beginners – the feeling that they have to play every hand they are dealt. This is because they may get impatient or feel somewhat left out if they don't play, or perhaps they don't want to look like a wuss in front of their mates. Of course, it could also be that they simply don't know any better. If you don't have an understanding of selecting a good starting hand, any hand that has a jack, queen, king or ace in it is going to look good.

There is an inherent problem with playing too many hands and that is that you are only going to hit the flop on a small number of times and, if you do hit the flop, it is still difficult to know if you have the best hand or not. Until you have an understanding of how to play beyond the cards in your hand, you will be playing n what you are dealt and, if you get involved in a large number of pots, your chips will be gone before you know it.

Playing with fear

While there are those players who play recklessly, there are others that are playing with fear. Having a lack of experience and not having played too many hands, a beginner poker player is often too afraid that they are going to make a mistake and look bad or they are just too frightened of losing. Because of this, many beginners will simply fold until they have a hand they know is unbeatable. Fear also plays a part in this and it can turn into paranoia very quickly. A paranoid player will automatically assume that any player who is aggressive in their betting must have a much better hand ad will fold all of their hands except for the absolute best. There is only one way to overcome this – get in some time at the tables and spend time on learning how to trust your own instincts.

Committing yourself to a hand

Poker is a very competitive game and, because of this, many players believe that it is not a good thing to give up. While you should never be a passive player, poker is not like all those other sports and it is often the right thing to do to fold your hand. When you first begin to play poker, it is very easy to let emotion get in the way. You may have a pocket pair pre flop or are looking to make a pair on the flop and, because you don't want an opponent t bluff you out of the pot, or because you don't want to seem weak, you stay in. Of course, the competitor inside of you could be telling you that you won't win if you fold. Sadly, by always calling bets, you never have a clue of where you in the hand until it are too late.

Making the wrong bet sizes

This is usually n no limit or pot limit games and we talked at length about this earlier. You must understand how to size a bet properly if you want to manipulate the table into dong what you want. Unfortunately, this is something that only comes with experience. There are some very common mistakes that can be easy to fi though. Many new players either bet too little or too much, usually when they want to raise the minimum pre-flop in a no limit game, when several players have already gone into the pot, or perhaps raising by five or six x the blind size when you are under the gun.

Improper bet sizing tends to happen after the flop as well. A beginner player will bet the minimum amount with a large hand, perhaps a set or two pairs, where there is already a lot of player sin. This gives them a cheap draw to a better hand. On the other hand, a beginner may also bet too much to try to protect what they see as a good hand. Both of these methods are wrong. In poker, the ideal situation is to bet a sufficient amount to maximize your potential winnings and minimize potential losses.

Chasing

This is similar to mistake number three. A beginner may stay in a hand in the hope that the community cards will improve things for them. They could be looking for flush draws or straights but are also betting to try to pair up an ace or another card for a two pair. It isn't always wrong to call on a draw but beginners tend to chase improper pot odds to do it. You might hit the cards you want but if you are chasing with improper odds, you will lose out in the long run.

Putting too much value on marginal hands

An extremely common mistake is playing a hand that might look god but actually holds little to no value or is very easily dominated. Examples of this include face cards or suited cards with bad kickers, i.e. king, five, or queen, three. This can also go for high hand combos like queen, ten, ace, nine or king, jack for example. While it doesn't necessarily follow that these hands can't be played, it takes experience to know how to play them. The real challenge with face cards is that there are few flops that will make you confident of having the top hand. Even if you do manage to pull a pair, you can very easily be booted or beaten by a higher value pair.

Letting emotion get in the way

We all have bad days, whether at work, home or on the table The trick is not to let those emotions get in the way of your decision making because this will turn into unprofitable action, like making desperate moves or chasing after big losses, not to mention letting your go stand in your way. Beginners may make rash moves, decisions based on emotion that prevent them from seeing everything that is going on, all they need to make the right decision. If you feel as though your emotions are taking over, it's time to step out and reset your emotions before you make a monumental mistake.

Playing out of your position

There are lots of things that go into your decisions in poker, beyond the cards you are holding. One of those factors is the position you are in, in relation to the order of the action. If you can act last, you can see how everyone is playing and what he or she are doing before you make your decision and this is one of the most powerful concepts in poker. However, beginners tend to make the mistake of entering the pot or calling a raise without any plan and out of position. Because they don't have the information they need, they get lost in the hand and that can lead to losses, not wins.

Too much bluffing

There are those players who believe that all you have to do in a hand of poker is bluff. Yes, it can be satisfying to successfully bluff an opponent out of the pot but you do need to make sure you are not too predictable. If you want your bluff to work, the other players need to believe that you have a top hand. If you bluff all the time, they will start to become unbelievable and no one will fall for them. Another part to bluffing is that your bet sizes have to match your bluff story to be believable.

Playing above what your bankroll says you can

Even if you play poker for fun, you should still have a bankroll. Many beginners don't understand how variance affects poker – you could be playing some great poker but still find yourself losing quite a lot. If you don't manage your bankroll, and stick to your limits, you will very quickly lose all the money. You may develop the skills to play at a higher level but if the bankroll isn't there, you won't be able to withstand the variance that will come at you – that will leave you broke.

Chapter 18

Life Affirming Truths for Poker

There are certain truths that you follow in life. You can use these truths even when you play poker! It is surprising, is it not? Let us get to it!

Make sure that you know yourself

This is something that every person believes. There are many books that motivate you to learn who you are. There are some people who have an outrageous image on the poker table. This image may work for many people at the table. There are other players who are better suited to playing cash games. You have to learn who you are. Always do what you do best! If there is a particular strategy that everybody is trying, you do not have to use it. You can use this strategy only if you think it will work for you.

You need to be responsible

You need to remember that what you achieve in life or in poker is what you deserve. You always receive what you need. You have to remember that in life it is karma that gives you what you deserve. You need to remember that what goes around comes around. It is the same when it comes to poker. You only gain what you have played for. If luck favors you too often you may earn some more. You need to make yourself accountable for whatever the outcome may be.

You need to think

As mentioned earlier, you have to ensure that you read up about poker, you will need to keep yourself right on top of the literature that is released. You need to always analyze the game. You could do it after the game is up or even when you are away from the game!

Always plan

You will need to plan. In life, you ensure that you have a plan every step of the way. You will need to have a similar plan when you decide to become a poker player. You will need to identify what your goal is. Did you always want to play poker? Why? Is it because you want to have fun? Is it because you want to break even? Have you dreamt of being the best player there ever was? Have you ever wanted to be a tournament player? If you find yourself without a plan, you need to worry! This is because of the fact that you are now someone else's plan!

Set deadlines for yourself

In life, you set yourself a schedule where you make note of what you need to do. It is only when you do this that you understand what it is that you need to achieve. You will need to plan for your games in advance. You have to ensure that you have deadlines. If you have a goal where you need to play for a minimum of two hours every day of every week, you have to work on doing that. You will need to ensure that you have a track of what your deadlines are. Make sure that your deadlines are realistic!

Be realistic

You should never have goals that do not make sense to you! You need to have reachable goals. If you are a person who fails in Math, you cannot give yourself the goal to pass Math in the next test! You will have to set goals for yourself, but it is your duty to ensure that these goals are reachable. You will have to keep trying. You should however not dream of winning the World Series of Poker this year if you have just started learning how to play.

You have to expect difficulties

When you are learning, you will fall prey to the flaws that you possess when it comes to poker. This is the same with life as well. When you are working on something for the first time, you will find that you are unable to get rid of your old habits. You may begin to procrastinate! It is true that you will take time to rise up to the top when it comes to poker or anything in life. Every person who has reached the top has struggled. They fell down but they rose again. This is what you must do too!

Always remember to Have Fun!

You have to enjoy yourself every step of the way! Imagine if you were living life in a sad manner. You will never have friends. You will also find yourself worried and sad. There are quite a few ups and downs that you will face in life. You have to celebrate all the ups! You will feel bad about the downs that you have faced but that are not the end of the world. You have to do the same in poker! You have to enjoy yourself when you play. What is the point of playing a game if you do not like it? If that is the case, you should find another game to play. Find something you would love to do. That way it would not be a waste of your time or your money! Make sure that you are always happy!

All the best!

Ian Dunross

Conclusion

Thank you once again for purchasing this book. Just to reiterate, there are only certain situations where you can bluff. As you keep playing the game, you will be able to identify these situations with increasing ease. Most beginners try to bluff as often as possible. This is wrong as it becomes predictable after a certain point and your opponents can easily call your bluffs. Bluffing effectively and efficiently is a key aspect of mastering poker.

There are different rules that you will need to abide by when you are playing poker. You could be banned or suspended from approaching the different poker rooms, either online or offline. There are different etiquettes that you need to follow too. These have been mentioned in the second chapter. You have to ensure that you abide by the etiquette as well.

There are different myths to poker like there are for every form of art. These myths had been spread by the people who believed that poker is a bad game, but this is highly untrue. This is because Poker is good for you! You learn more about how you should think strategically. You need to remember that you do not need to be great at math or statistics to okay poker. All you need is the right strategy at the right time.

Besides bluffing, other key aspects such as reading your opponents need to be learnt before you can play a high stakes poker game. It is advisable to first play poker for a few months without real money. You can find such environments online or you could just play with friends or family. Once you think you are good enough, you can step out into the real world of poker.

Made in the USA
Middletown, DE
23 October 2015